Rapha's Handbook *for* Group Leaders

Revised Edition

Rapha's Handbook *for* Group Leaders

Revised Edition

Richard Price
Pat Springle

Rapha Publishing
Houston, TX

Rapha's Handbook for Group Leaders, 2d ed.
by Richard Price and Pat Springle

Second printing
ISBN: 0-945276-42-7
Printed in the United States of America

Contents

Acknowledgments

THANKS TO Sandy Ballard, Stuart Rothberg, Joe Kloba, Rujon Morrison, Sharlene Johnson, and Robert Pace for their contributions to this material.

Introduction

God has used small groups throughout history to influence people's lives. We see this most clearly in the ministry of Jesus Christ. Even though He ministered to the masses, He also sought to develop the faith of the twelve disciples in the context of a small group. After His earthly ministry, Jesus' early followers continued this use of groups. For example, Paul trained small groups of leaders as he founded churches throughout Asia Minor and Greece.

After the establishment of Christianity, God continued to use group environments to effect change in His people's lives. In England, for example, John Wesley established a renewal movement through his use of "societies" and "bands," small groups of people formed to sustain personal Christian growth.

Today, the need for effective small groups has increased. Our mobile, urban society creates a longing in people to belong. People who move, on average, once every two to three years and whose extended families are separated by hundreds of miles possess a need to be involved significantly with other people. They need the support of others who care for them; they need to belong to a group of people who knows and loves them.

The needs evident in modern society and God's historical use of the small group environment provide ample justification for your desire to be an effective group leader. Leading others in a discovery of God's truth and what it can mean for their lives is an exciting opportunity. Yet, in the words of one experienced group leader, the new leader often experiences "self-doubt, anxiety, and downright trepidation." *Rapha's Handbook for Group Leaders* is designed to help you overcome these roadblocks so that you will feel comfortable, equipped, and adequate for the job of leading a group of people in this discovery.

MEETING THE "FELT" NEEDS OF PEOPLE

This handbook addresses the full spectrum of types of groups, but it is specifically designed to provide resources for leaders of growth and support groups. These groups focus upon the emotional, relational, and spiritual needs of people. People attend growth and support groups because the groups are designed to minister to their felt needs. The circumstances of their lives may have produced hurt, anger, loss, disappointment, or abuse. Most encounter very difficult circumstances which result from their misguided choices. Many experience the effects of other people's irresponsibilty. All are seeking solutions and hope. As a result, we expect that you will deal with people's feelings, choices, and relationships during the course of your group.

Many people are wary of starting groups in their churches which deal with people's emotional issues. One newcomer to a growth group commented, "We ought to be dealing exclusively with God's Word and drop this attention on family background and emotions. We're just selling out to the world." Indeed, some groups have given little attention to biblical guidance and have encouraged a drift away from the Word of God. In these cases, suspicion is justified.

However, when biblical content is properly applied to people's emotional lives, this concern subsides. Many Christians believe that our knowledge of the truth is the only thing that should influence our behavior. In reality, what we feel influences what we do almost as much as what we believe. Christianity is not simply a matter of thinking and doing. Nor should we merely feel and do. Rather, we should think, feel, and do. For example, if we emotionally experience the love of God in addition to mentally believing in His love, we will act in ways that demonstrate the truth that God is loving. David confessed, "Surely you [God] desire truth in the inner parts; you teach me wisdom in the inmost place" (Psalm 51:6). These "inner parts" include our emotions. When handled in this fashion, the acknowledgement of our emotional lives can be rich and profitable.

One pastor voiced deep disappointment over his life and ministry. He recalled his initial calling to ministry and described how those early dreams had not come true. He said, "I know God causes all things to work together for good for me. I know He cares for me. I just don't feel it." He was experiencing a conflict between what he knew to be true and what he felt to be true. Admirably, he still chose to believe in God's loving concern for him. Yet, in the depths of his heart, he lacked the assurance that God really cared, and his behavior showed it. He represents thousands of people who will benefit from dealing with difficult circumstances from a thorough and biblical perspective.

The information found in this handbook will help you begin to lead others in applying God's truth to the deepest parts of their lives. It will not train you to be a counselor. Nor do we expect you to become one. In fact, you may encounter situations when you need to refer a group member to someone trained in professional counseling. Yet, you will find insights into why people believe one thing and do another in spite of their beliefs, and you will discover ways to help them live more genuinely.

EXCESSES AND REACTIONS

Virtually every successful movement spawns excesses and subsequent reactions to these excesses. For instance, the "Jesus Movement" on campuses during the 60s was used by God to lead hundreds of thousands to Christ, but the enthusiasm for discipleship also led to cults like David Berg's "Children of God." The church growth movement began as an attempt to heighten the public's awareness of the faith and draw people into churches, but some proponents focused exclusively on secular marketing techniques to attract people at the expense of a proper emphasis on faith and the Holy Spirit's power to draw people into the family of God.

The small group movement's powerful ministry to hurting people has also bred a number of excesses. Several magazine articles and books have identified and criticized them. These sources accurately cite the spurious theology and anthropology in the writings and teachings of those who try to comfort hurting people with the affirmation that "man is good, so you are good," and "the real you is perfect." These and many other pop psychology themes have no basis in solid biblical teaching of the fallen nature of man, the love and grace of God, His forgiveness, and our new identity in Christ.

Critics claim that the recovery/support group movement promotes wallowing in victimization, encourages blaming others for our faults, and absolves people of personal responsibility. The more theological critics point out the half-truths of those who claim the central theme of the Bible is: "Christ came to meet needs." Certainly, Christ came to meet our needs, but our paramount need is to be forgiven and given new life and purpose. Some of us, however, communicate that Christ came primarily to make us happier. He can then be reduced to a God to be used for our purposes instead of a God to be worshipped, appreciated, and followed for His purposes.

Where these fallacies and half-truths are communicated, we agree with the critics. These views and methods are wrong! But we are careful to point out that these are the excesses, not the norm. We don't "throw out the baby with the bath water." We need perception, truth, and balance.

The process of emotional healing from abuse or abandonment is not as quick and simple as many of the critics claim, however. The clear fact is: many people *are* victims, and the early stages of recovery involve breaking through the wall of denial so that the wounds can be exposed. That exposure allows long-repressed hurt and anger to surface, and many people looking in from the outside are not comfortable with those emotions. They would rather these victims continued to repress their painful feelings.

TRUE RECOVERY

True recovery involves the exposure of the victim's wounds, but it also involves the grieving of those wounds and acting responsibly in our behavior and relationships. Recovery necessarily involves both grief and repentance: grieving the wounds caused by the sins of others, and repentance for our own sinful behavior, such as bitterness, abuse, and withdrawal.

Recovery also involves a change in our view of God. "Christ came to meet needs" sounds very attractive to those who have doubted His essential goodness, but it doesn't mean that He is obligated to give us a loving spouse, kind parents, money, health, and happiness. God may give those to us if He chooses, but He may not. (Read Heb. 11:32-38 for examples of those who God delivered and those who continued to suffer.) The Scriptures clearly state, however, that God does provide the essential elements for an "abundant life": His wisdom, love, forgiveness, strength, and "precious and magnificent promises," no matter what our circumstances are.

What, then, is the purpose of groups? How do they fit into God's plan for His people? These groups provide a nurturing environment for people to grow in their love for God and obedience to Him. In this atmosphere, they can honestly appraise the wounds and hindrances in their lives. They can then grieve and make better choices. The Westminster Catechism proclaims: "The chief end of man is to glorify God and enjoy Him forever." Paul echoed that thought in 1 Cor. 10:31 where he encouraged the Corinthian believers to "do all to the glory of God." Honoring Christ does not mean denying emotional pain, looking for quick fixes, or wallowing in victimization and blame. Instead, it means learning to profoundly apply God's Word to real life.

GROUPS IN THE CHURCH

We believe the small groups which function in a local church should do so under the leadership of that church. In many churches, the leadership already has a policy which guides the nature and growth of the church's small group ministry. As a result, we encourage those who want to start groups to approach their church's small group coordinator or their pastor about their desire.

This handbook and our materials do not depend upon any particular guiding policy for church small group ministries. The only natural condition is that the church leadership recognize the need to minister to people's personal, emotional, relational, and spiritual needs in the context of small groups.

In cases when a church does not have a guiding policy for the entire spectrum of task groups, fellowship groups, discipleship groups, growth groups and support groups, we suggest the training provided by Serendipity House (Littleton, Colorado). In his *Training Manual for Groups*, Lyman Coleman describes 15 models of successful small groups currently in use by a variety of churches. He further provides an annotated bibliography by Dr. Roberta Hestenes and suggestions for developing a small group ministry.

LEGAL CONCERNS

Some churches are concerned about the risk of litigation if a group member exhibits destructive behavior. This risk will be minimized if the promotion about the groups states that they are lay-led growth or support groups. Group members need to know that leaders and facilitators do not assume professional responsibility for the group members. Other factors which limit a church's legal liability for small groups include:

- Instruct the leaders and facilitators to refrain from offering direct, drastic advice such as, "You ought to divorce that irresponsible husband of yours!"
- Do not charge for groups (except, of course, for the materials covered in the group, and possibly, the refreshments).
- Have the church's small group coordinator shepherd the leaders and facilitators to assure quality leadership and to help them know when to refer someone to a professional.
- Have a system of referral so that people with depressive or destructive behaviors can readily get the help they need.

By observing these guidelines, the church should have very little risk of litigation regarding its small group ministry.

Rapha Resources constantly provides new resources for group leaders and facilitators. We also offer an audio tape series which complements this handbook. For a free catalog of our materials and prices, please call 1-800-460-HOPE.

The Goals and Expectations of a Group

OBJECTIVES

- to help you understand the uniquenesses of various types of groups which can be used in the church,
- to provide an understanding of the specific goals for growth and support groups, and
- to provide realistic expectations for you as you lead people through the healing process.

SMALL GROUPS ARE PART OF the fabric of our everyday lives. Many of us car pool, eat meals, work, study, and socialize in small groups. Some groups are formal, others are informal, some are binding and permanent, others are flexible and temporary. Few of us are untouched by small groups.

Rarely do we consider the purpose and goals of these groups, yet they usually function quite well. They succeed largely because they are such a familiar part of our lives. We enter meetings at work knowing the purpose is to accomplish a certain task. We attend parties with the understanding that the goal is to have fun.

It is not always necessary to discuss the rationale for a group for that group to succeed. On the other hand, a clear understanding of a group's reason for existence can greatly enhance its effectiveness. This is especially true when people encounter a new kind of group, either as a leader or as a member. Knowledge of a group's purpose enables the people involved to adjust their expectations and behavior. Without this knowledge, the group may lack cohesiveness and direction.

Types of Small Groups

Task groups exist to accomplish a certain project, whether it is organizing a retreat, selecting new church furnishings, or planning a worship service. Church committees and boards are usually task groups.

Fellowship groups are sponsored by many churches. These neighborhood fellowship groups have very little didactic content, but they include a lot of interaction and prayer. These groups are primarily designed to help people get to know each other in an informal setting. As relationships develop, fellowship groups may evolve into a higher commitment and become teaching groups or growth groups.

Teaching groups communicate knowledge and information largely through the lecture method of instruction. Most youth classes and almost all adult Sunday School classes and education programs fit into this type of group. Discipleship groups may also fall under this category, though these have more emphasis on application.

Many successful churches are incorporating two additional types of groups in their ministries.

Growth groups are designed to make people more aware of felt-needs and strained relationships. Growth group leaders create an environment to encourage and challenge members to grow in their personal, relational, and spiritual lives. They tend to focus upon a program of content which encourages them to grow in areas such as marriage, family and work life, self-esteem, and codependency. Churches may choose to begin their support group ministry by starting growth groups. After the ministry has been established, growth groups continue to be an optional entry point for people who are first joining groups.

Each of our groups is built around a book that forms the basis of the group discussions. Our growth groups are based on a 13- or 14-week format. For those groups, we have small group leader's guides available.

Support groups, which focus upon specific emotional or relational needs, are being used by many churches. Generally, members attend because they feel stress in coping with life's problems. People attend because they need support and perspective in dealing, for example, with codependency, eating disorders, sexual abuse, grief, job loss, divorce recovery, alcohol or drug abuse, or single-parenting. Support groups are led by facilitators who promote mutual help and support. Our support groups, such as Victims of Sexual Abuse and 12-Steps for Chemical Dependency, Codependency, and Eating Disorders, provide material for a 6-month to 2-year support group format.

Each of these groups serves a useful function in the life of the church. Yet, they must be used appropriately. For example, those who are assigned the task of maintaining the church property would be poorly advised to select anything other than a task group approach. The types of groups employed must meet the existing needs.

One helpful way to understand the similarities and differences between these groups is to examine them in light of four major activities of groups. For example, teaching groups engage in the dispensing of information and task groups devote most of their time to planning action or actually working on projects. The following chart summarizes these activities.

ACTIVITY	FOCUSES ON	EXAMPLES
giving information	what you should know	public lectures, Sunday School classes
encouraging discussion	what you think	home Bible studies, town meetings
facilitating process	what you feel	counseling groups, grief support groups
planning action	what you do	committee meetings, workshops

The following chart describes the four types of groups in light of these four activities.

	TYPES OF GROUPS			
Activities	**Task**	**Teaching**	**Growth**	**Support**
giving information	medium	high	low	low
encouraging discussion	medium	low	high	high
facilitating process	none	none	medium	high
planning action	high	low	medium	medium

For example, a teaching group will be high on communicating information, low on discussion and action, and give very little or no attention to processing how the members feel about the information. On the other hand, support groups give just enough information to facilitate high degrees of discussion and process. The primary place for action lies in the everyday lives of the members, not in the group meeting itself.

Many people, Christians and non-Christians alike, need the environment provided by growth and support groups. This is largely due to the erosion of social and family support networks in America's mobile society. The church stands in a unique position to provide light and hope to people in our society who encounter life's difficulties.

Goals For Growth and Support Groups

Growth and support groups provide powerful, reflective, nurturing environments in which God can change lives. In this context, people can learn to grieve their losses and take responsibility for their feelings, behavior, and desires. This objective applies to all of Rapha's materials. In addition to this broad objective, each group topic will chart its own specific objectives. These narrower objectives define more specifically the ways in which people can change. Whatever the specific objectives may be, every activity, every discussion, and every interaction should provide opportunities for people to trust and choose wisely.

Through His Word we know that God wants to change His people, but He does not change everybody to the same degree and in the same way. Some people will change dramatically during the course of your group. Others will change in small ways. Still others may not change at all. Their growth is not your responsibility. The responsibility for growth lies with God. You simply provide the nurturing environment in which God can cause growth to occur (1 Corinthians 3:5–9).

Use of Rapha's Resources

Many people have used Rapha's growth and support group materials in already existing large group functions such as Sunday School classes, evening church training programs, and women's ministry programs. While these traditional activities generally follow a lecture style, many have found the transition to a discussion format well-received by the people in their groups. In addition, our growth group materials provide lesson plans for 13 group discussions, so they easily fit into the quarterly programming of the church.

These materials have also been used effectively in a variety of environments, including retreats, seminars, and women's studies where a combination of large group teaching and small group formatting is used. In addition, these small groups can provide a church with the tools for an effective, needs-oriented community outreach strategy.

You can use Rapha's materials with a group which traditionally has been a teaching group by making a few modifications. This handbook is designed for use in growth and support groups, yet certain techniques of interactive small group leadership can be applied in a teaching group. For example, by using the material on effective discussion questions, you can increase the amount and quality of class discussion and, thus, improve your class's understanding and application of the content.

Your church may already have several small groups functioning. Rapha's materials are a natural fit in these situations. For example, you may belong to a small group Bible study discussion that meets on Tuesday evenings. You could study the doctrines of salvation and how they relate to one's self-esteem (via *The Search for Significance*) during the Fall, and return to a study of Colossians in the Spring. You may, however, choose to continue to pursue the applications of Scripture to felt-needs by studying books like *Your Parents and You* or *Codependency: A Christian Perspective*.

You may also want to start a group from the ground up. Often, people want to get to know others in the church outside the already existing programs. They may desire a more relaxed atmosphere and more time to talk with people and share their struggles, experiences, and insights. Because our material encourages personal interaction in addition to biblical input, these people can find the place where they can get to know others on a more intimate and personal level.

Many churches are developing recovery ministries to help minister more specifically and effectively to hurting people. Rapha's materials are designed to equip leaders and facilitators to provide powerful and nurturing environments.

The books and workbooks used in these groups expose hurt and anger, providing hope and healing for deep wounds and strained relationships.

Realistic Expectations

Often people have unrealistic expectations about their emotional growth and healing. Some believe any progress is utterly hopeless; others think they can quickly and easily get over deep wounds and complex problems. People need to see themselves "in the process," encouraged and strengthened by a support system, God's strength, and a sense of patience.

A SUPPORT SYSTEM

As the person experiences the new sensation of people asking caring questions instead of demanding his instant rescuing, he will begin to feel valued as a person. As he takes the risk of being honest about his weaknesses and sins, he can experience the forgiveness and acceptance of others (especially yours). As people listen to him without correcting him, he will gain confidence. As others let him make his own decisions, feel his own feelings, and think his own thoughts, he will gain a new sense of strength. As people genuinely care for him, he will learn to experience authentic love. He will begin to believe that God isn't harsh or aloof as he originally thought. He will begin to genuinely experience the tender, strong, consistent love of God for him. And he will then learn to express that love to others.

GOD'S ENABLEMENT

The truths we have examined can have tremendous implications on our every goal and relationship, but now we need to understand how to actually implement them in our lives. How can we begin to experience positive change? Jesus answered this question in His last time of intimate instruction with His disciples (John 13–16). He told them that He would soon be put to death, but that they would not be left alone: "And I will ask the Father, and He will give you another Helper, that He may be with you forever" (John 14:16). That Helper is the Holy Spirit, who came some fifty days later to direct and empower the believers at Pentecost. That same Holy Spirit indwells each believer today, and serves as our instructor, counselor, and source of spiritual power as we live for Christ's glory and honor.

Who is the Holy Spirit, and why did He come? The Holy Spirit, the third Person of the Trinity, is God and possesses all the attributes of deity. His primary purpose is to glorify Christ and bring attention to Him. Christ said, "He shall glorify Me; for He shall take of Mine, and shall disclose it to you" (John 16:14). The Holy Spirit is our teacher, and He guides us into the truth of the Scriptures (John 16:13). It is by His power that the love of Christ flows through us and produces spiritual fruit within us (John 7:37–39; 15:1–8). This spiritual fruit is described in many ways in the New Testament, including: intimate friendship with Christ (John 15:14); love for one another (John 15:12); joy and peace in the midst of difficulties (John 14:27; 15:11); steadfastness (Ephesians 5:18–21); and evangelism and discipleship (Matthew 28:18–20).

Obviously, this fruit is not always evident in the lives of Christians, but why not? As we all know, the Christian life is not an easy one. It is not simply a self-improvement program. True, we may at times be able to make some changes in our habits through our own discipline and determination, but Christianity is not merely self-effort. The Christian life is a supernatural one in which we draw on Christ as our resource for direction, encouragement, and strength.

TIME

If we were computers, solutions to our problems would be produced in microseconds. People, however, don't change that quickly. The agrarian metaphors given in the Scriptures depict seasons of planting, weeding, watering, growth, and harvesting. Farmers don't expect to plant seeds in the morning and harvest their crops that afternoon. Seeds must go through a complete cycle of growth, receiving plenty of attention in the process, before they mature. In this age of instant coffee, microwave dinners, and instant banking, we tend to assume that spiritual, emotional, and relational health will be instantaneous. These unrealistic expectations only cause discouragement and disappointment.

Although this book's primary focus is on the cognitive, or right-thinking, aspect of our spiritual growth, we need to remember that all of these elements are required to produce growth and health. Our growth will be stunted and superficial if we don't give proper emphasis to honesty about our emotions, affirming relationships, right thinking promoted through biblical study and application, the ministry of the Holy Spirit, and time.

Some of us seem to respond to this environment of growth very quickly; others, after a few weeks or months; and still others, never at all. Why the difference? Why are some of us able to apply principles of growth so much more readily than others? The answer is that differing factors will produce a variety of responses from different people. Those who respond quickly may not be as wounded as others, or they may already be in an environment which has prepared them for relatively rapid growth.

Some of us are in situations where one or more elements of growth are in some way missing or lacking. We may be trying to deal with our difficulties alone. We may be depending on a rigid structure of discipline for positive change, instead of blending a healthy combination of our responsibility with the Holy Spirit's enabling power. We may be expecting too much too soon, and may be experiencing disappointment with our slow results. Some of us may, in fact, be ready to quit the growth process entirely.

Those of us who can't seem to get the light turned on have the greatest difficulty in beginning this process. We can't see our problems. We may recognize that something is wrong, but can't pinpoint exactly what. Or, our defense mechanisms of denial may be so strong that we're unable to see any needs in our lives at all.

A young man asked me, "What about people from very stable backgrounds? They don't wrestle with the difficulties you're talking about, do they?"

"All of us have a fallen, sinful nature," I responded. "Because of that, we all wrestle to some degree with the fears of failure and rejection, and with feelings of inadequacy, guilt, and shame. Those from stable, loving families are usually better able to determine what their difficulties are and be honest about them, than those who are shackled by the defense mechanisms that are often developed in dysfunctional families.

"Those from abusive, manipulative, or neglectful families have far more to overcome than those from a healthier home environment," I explained. "Alcoholism, divorce, sexual abuse, physical abuse, workaholism, drug abuse, and other major family disorders leave deep wounds. Many people from backgrounds like these have suppressed their intense hurt and anger for so long that they are simply out of touch with the reality in their lives. Therefore, just as a broken arm requires more time, attention, and therapy for healing than does a small abrasion, people suffering from deep emotional, spiritual, and relational injuries need more time, attention, love, and encouragement than those with more minor wounds. Though the process for recovery may take longer, enjoying health in these areas is still possible if all the elements of healing are applied over its duration."

Another person asked, "Why doesn't just understanding these issues work? Why isn't knowledge enough to produce change?"

"Man is a relational, physical, emotional, and spiritual being," I said. "We develop and learn and grow best in an environment of honesty, love, and affirmation, where all aspects of our nature are given the encouragement to heal."

A woman asked me, "What do I need to do to begin seeing some results?"

"Put yourself in an environment of growth, which includes all the elements of honesty, affirming relationships, right thinking, the ministry of the Holy Spirit, and time. I can't tell you how or when growth will come—but I know that it will come if you are patient and persistent."

A businessman asked, "Why do I not see much change in my life?" After talking with him for awhile, three issues surfaced which can be common to many of us: First, this gentleman had advanced significantly in his profession by performing well and pleasing people. Although he had received promotions, raises, prestige, and comfort, he still wasn't happy. Yet, it was difficult for him to consider living by a pattern of behavior other than that which had seemingly brought him so far.

In addition, this man was afraid of how he might respond to the generosity of God's love and freedom. He feared that he would either abuse God's grace or be so changed by it that some of his friends and business associates might make fun of him and ultimately reject him.

Finally, he feared that if he did respond wholeheartedly to God's love, the Lord might test his faith by making his life miserable. "I couldn't stand that," he told me. "My life is painful now, but at least I'm used to it. If I surrender completely to God, my life might get totally out of control."

These and many other reasons make the process of spiritual, relational, emotional, and mental health elusive to many people. But again, honesty is our starting point. When we are willing to be open about our thoughts and fears, we generally find that others have thought and felt much the same way.

Our growth toward wholeness and maturity is a journey which won't be completed until we join the Lord in heaven. The Apostle Paul understood this, and saw himself as being in the middle of this process. He wrote to the Philippian believers:

> Not that I have already obtained it, or have already become perfect, but I press on in order that I may lay hold of that for which I was laid hold of by Christ Jesus.
>
> Philippians 3:12

If Paul, the foremost missionary and writer of much of the New Testament, saw himself as being "in the process," we can be encouraged to continue in the process toward change as well. It will help to have reasonable expectations about our progress. Sometimes, we will experience flashes of insight and spurts of growth, but the process of healing and renewal will more often be slow and methodical. Our emotions, too, may occasionally be very pleasant and positive, but when God's light shines on another area of hurt in our lives, we will likely experience another round of pain and anger. Remember that healing can only continue as we put ourselves in an environment characterized by honesty, affirming relationships, right thinking, the Holy Spirit's love and power, and time.*

Evaluation Questions

1. Think back on the groups of which you have been a member in the past. What types of groups were they? What purposes do you think the group leader had for the group?

* *The Search for Significance,* 2d ed., Robert S. McGee (Houston, TX: Rapha Publishing, 1990) pp. 34–37.

Use the chart below and describe these groups. For example, your most recent group may have been a missions group which was high on giving content, low on encouraging discussion and process, and medium on planning action.

Name of Recent Group:	Missions Committee		
Giving information:	high		
Encouraging discussion:	low		
Facilitating process:*	low		
Planning action:	medium		

Remember: process refers to working through the *why's, how's, when's,* and *what's* of emotions.

Also, think back on the groups of which you have *led* in the past. What types of groups were they? What objectives did you set for the group? Did you meet your objectives? Why, or why not?

. Read 1 Corinthians 3:5–9. What is your responsibility as you lead your group?

What is God's responsibility?

How does this affect your confidence in leading the group? Does it increase or decrease your stress? Why?

3. Many new group leaders are anxious about leading their first group. Others are even terrified. What feelings do you have about leading your next group? Describe what makes you feel this way.

4. What are some creative ways your church can move into the arena of felt-needs groups?

5. What are your goals for your group? What are your personal goals for developing as a group leader?

6. Do you tend to have unrealistic expectations about how your group will bond, communicate, and grow? If so, what are they, and how will you deal with them?

Organization and Selection

OBJECTIVE

- to suggest a simple organizational structure for a small group ministry, and
- to provide criteria for selecting a coordinator, group leaders, and facilitators.

Organizing Your Group Ministry

As we mentioned in chapter 1, you may already have several small groups at your church. You can explain the variety of groups Rapha offers and let the leaders of those groups choose to use our materials if they desire. You may also have people who want to begin new groups. Some of these may be specific, need-oriented groups, so these leaders may want to use our materials dealing with these issues (such as chemical dependency, codependency, sexual abuse, grief, divorce, anorexia, bulimia, and compulsive overeating). If you or your group leaders are unsure of which material to teach, consider *The Search for Significance* as the starting group material. This can be followed by *Your Parents and You*, *Codependency: A Christian Perspective*, *Getting Unstuck*, or any of our other materials.

For instance, you may have one or more growth groups using *The Search for Significance* for a quarter, then your groups can expand to include our other growth group materials for the next quarter. Next, several people may surface who want to lead ongoing support groups. They can be trained and support groups can then be added to the variety of nurturing, small group environments within your church.

We recommend that churches with little or no support group experience focus on establishing a strong growth group ministry. After several quarters, perhaps some of these leaders can become support group facilitators, or other capable people can be found. Also, we recommend that groups have co-leaders and co-facilitators to share in the teaching and grooming of more people to become good leaders and facilitators.

Organizational Structure

INITIAL ORGANIZATIONAL STRUCTURE

It is important to select a competent and qualified coordinator for your group ministry. The coordinator, then, will be responsible for selecting and training people to lead the groups. At first, the organization of the small groups in your church may look like this:

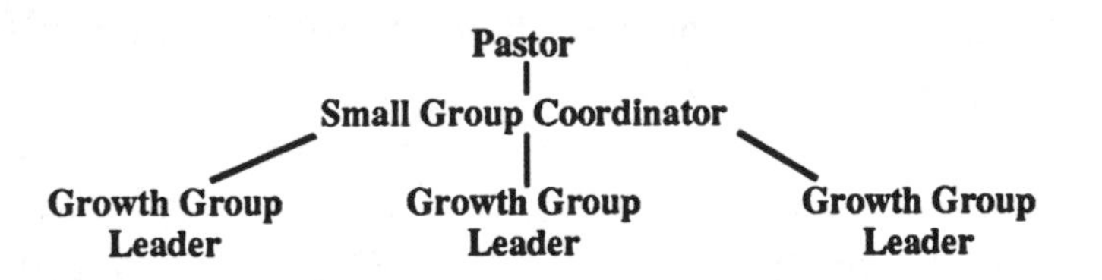

ADVANCED ORGANIZATIONAL STRUCTURE

Later, as more groups are formed, your church may need an assistant to help train and shepherd more group leaders. (If you plan to start with more than four or five groups, you may need to have an assistant coordinator from the outset.) The organization then may look like this:

Pastor

Small Group Coordinator — Assistant Coordinator

GGL GGL GGL GGL GGL GGL — SGF SGF SGF SGF SGF SGF

GGL - Growth Group Leader **SGF - Support Group Facilitator**

Or the coordinator and his assistant can divide responsibilities. For example, the coordinator can focus on the selection and training of leaders and facilitators while the assistant coordinator devotes his or her attention to problem-solving and encouragement.

The small group program can be a powerful ministry in your church if the groups are led by godly, competent leaders. The group leaders, in turn, need to be led by godly and competent small group coordinators. May the Lord guide you in your selection!

Selecting a Coordinator

Selecting leadership is an important step in the development of any organization. Success usually depends on the quality of the leaders. The success of this program may depend on your selection of a godly, qualified, and competent coordinator to oversee the small group ministry. This person may be a staff member, a deacon, an elder, or some other layperson. Both men and women may be considered.

Your church may already have a small group coordinator for fellowship and discipleship groups. If you now want to extend the ministry to include growth and support groups, you can incorporate these under the existing coordinator or select another person to specialize in these felt-need groups.

Instead of selecting a coordinator in the very beginning, you may wish to enlist several leaders and facilitators and then choose as your coordinator the one who emerges from the training as the real leader of the group. You will want someone who has the following qualifications.

- **Proven Spiritual Leadership** - Takes initiative; is skilled at selecting and shepherding others.
- **Good Relational Skills** - Merits the trust and respect of others; encourages others and speaks the truth in love.
- **Good Organizational Skills** - Able to plan, delegate, and follow through.

THE SMALL GROUP COORDINATOR'S JOB DESCRIPTION

- Select growth group leaders and support group facilitators (with input from the pastor).
- Participate in training leaders and facilitators.
- Lead the ongoing training and development of leaders and facilitators.
- Participate in problem solving.
- Shepherd and encourage the leaders and facilitators.
- Serve as an example of love, faith, strength, and prayer.
- Serve as a liaison to the pastor for the small group ministry.
- Arrange for referrals for those group participants who may need more help than the groups can provide.

The small group coordinator will play a vital role in beginning and maintaining groups in your church. In many churches, the coordinator will be a staff member (i.e., education, adult, or family minister). In other churches, he or she may be a key lay leader who has an avid interest in the ministry. The person chosen will serve as the liaison between the church staff and the small groups.

Selecting Leaders and Facilitators

The selection of leadership is the single most important factor which determines the success of small groups.

GROWTH GROUP LEADERS

One of the main tasks of the coordinator is the selection of qualified, competent, and teachable leaders and facilitators. Selecting the right growth group leaders and support group facilitators will make the difference between success and failure for the program. You are not looking for the perfect group leaders, but for leaders who have the following characteristics:

- **Faithful . . .** to prepare for the group meetings, to pray for the members of the group, and to lead the group with love and strength
- **Available . . .** to the group members, being honest and vulnerable with them
- **Teachable . . .** willing to learn from other small group leaders, trainers, group members, and the Lord. Previous experience leading small groups is beneficial for group leaders, but isn't necessary. Everybody has to start somewhere.

SUPPORT GROUP FACILITATORS

Generally, support groups are effective because the facilitator has personal experience in the recovery process. In addition to the qualities listed for growth group leaders, facilitators need significant experience in personal recovery and group work. We recommend for facilitators of . . .

. . . chemical dependency support groups, 2 years of sobriety and 2 years group experience

. . . eating disorder support groups (if possible, we recommend separate groups for anorexia, bulimia, and compulsive overeating), 2 years recovery and 2 years group experience

. . . **codependency support groups**, 2 years recovery, 1 year group experience

. . . **grief support groups**, 1 year in recovery, 1 year group experience

. . . **divorce recovery support groups**, 2 years in recovery, 1 year group experience

. . . **sexual abuse support groups**, master's degree in counseling with a specialty in working with sexually abused people

. . . **sexual addiction support groups**, master's degree in counseling with a specialty in working with sexually abused people

(***Note*:** Some have asked why we recommend people with a master's degree for sexual abuse and sexual addiction groups. The depth of the wounds and the volatility of the emotions require a facilitator who is skilled in handling difficult situations. Most lay counselors or facilitators are unskilled and unable to adequately minister in these extremely difficult situations. The choice of leadership of groups, however, is under the auspices of the local church.)

Evaluation Questions

1. Describe the current small group ministry at your church. (Consider: Who is the coordinator? What types of groups exist? What is their purpose, duration, and content? How are leaders selected and trained? How effective are these groups?)

2. What is the existing organizational structure?

3. What are your plans to use specific materials to move people through the healing process? (For instance, you may choose to start with *The Search for Significance*, then *Your Parents and You*, *Codependency: A Christian Perspective*, *Getting Unstuck*. At any point, someone may choose to join a support group to deal with specific issues.)

4. How will you (or your church) select and train leaders and facilitators?

5. What are the qualifications for the leaders or facilitators of each type of group?

6. What are some realistic expectations for this stage of your group ministry?
   (***Consider:*** How many leaders and their groups do you expect to succeed? . . . to struggle? What factors will encourage growth? . . . inhibit growth?)

The Mechanics of a Group

OBJECTIVES

- to help you determine the objectives, format, and content for each group meeting, and
- to provide practical suggestions for asking good questions.

EFFECTIVE GROUPS depend upon three major factors: the character of the group leader, the group skills developed by the leader, and the amount of attention given to the practical aspects of group leading. In this chapter, we will focus upon selecting objectives, formatting the meeting, and asking good questions.

The success of your group will depend in part upon the quality of your preparation. The time spent each week in preparation will vary depending upon your experience. Initially, your preparation will take an hour or two of your time. After you gain experience and feel more comfortable in your role, this investment of time will decrease.*

* For additional discussion of practical group leading suggestions for the local church, see *How To Lead Small Group Bible Studies* (Colorado Springs: NavPress, 1982) and *Small Group Leader's Handbook* (Downers Grove, IL: InterVarsity Press).

Selecting Your Objectives

You can increase the quality of your preparation by first gaining a broad perspective of the meeting. As you review the content for each week, ask yourself, *What do I want to accomplish with this content?* You can narrow the scope of this question by focusing upon the answers to three other questions: what do you want your group members to *know*, what do you want them to *feel*, and what do you want them to *do*. The answers to these questions should be fairly short and easily remembered.

What they know: Select the key idea for the week's discussion. Often leaders select too many ideas to discuss, and, consequently, the group lacks focus, often running overtime. Select one main idea, at the most two, upon which to focus.

What they feel: Ideas affect the way people think. Less obvious, but just as vital, is the concept that ideas also affect the way people feel. While feelings are never an adequate basis for authentic Christian living and while one should never encourage an emotionalism deficient in truth, emotions often reflect what we truly believe.

The biblical writers, especially the Hebrew poets, call upon the people of God to experience the truth of God. For example, David encourages his readers, "Taste and see that the Lord is good" (Psalms 34:8). Many Christians acknowledge that God is good, but few of them experience that goodness on an emotional level. As a result, they sense a conflict between what they know and what they feel. In moments of brutal honesty, as in response to significant adversity or loss, they will often say that they really do not believe in God's goodness even though they desperately want to. By selecting an affective (emotional) objective for the meeting, you can help your group members bridge the gap between what they know to be true and what they feel.

What they do: Truth calls for action. Yet, many of us behave no differently than the non-Christians around us. We are frequently as proud, spiteful, angry, manipulative, hopeless, and self-serving as those who do not know God. By encouraging your group to consider specific behavioral goals, group members will be motivated to live out what they say they believe.

Behavioral goals can be quite different for people in differing situations. For instance, Romans 12:9 says, "Let love be without hypocrisy." A person who typically withdraws can apply this passage by moving toward someone to develop a relationship. A codependent person, however, may realize that his or her "love" for others has been designed to control them. That behavior is hypocritical love, so this person may need to detach temporarily to assess motives in relationships. So application for some is to give, but for others it is to stop giving with hidden, selfish motives. For some it is to forgive, but for others it is to be honest about the repressed hurt, anger, and bitterness. This honesty can then lead to forgiveness. Behavioral goals need to be applied specifically and carefully in each person's life.

One practical way to grasp your objectives for the week is to think through the implications of the content. This allows you to anticipate the group members' responses as well as to suggest more significant applications. One way to think through the implications of the content is to ask yourself, *How would I respond to that point in a group? How would I feel? What would I want to do? What practical difference does it make?*

You will have time to think through implications if you prepare a week ahead of time. For example, on Wednesday begin reading the material for the next meeting on the following Tuesday. As you go through the week you will think of questions your members might have and ways to apply the concepts in everyday life.

Meeting Format

After you have a broad perspective of the objectives for the week, you can then fit your objectives into a specific plan of action. Many effective group leaders follow, at least loosely, a consistent format each week. The following format promotes natural interaction and has been used successfully by many leaders.

This format can be modified if you wish. Many successful groups switch the discussion and prayer time (the order then is mixing, opening, discussion, prayer, and closing). This modified format allows you to spend more time praying for one another's needs. (If you choose to provide more time for prayer or fellowship, be sure to set a time limit on the discussion.)

MIXING. As people arrive, help them feel welcome and at home. You might have some music playing in the background. Select music which is received well by the people in your group. For example, younger people in their thirties and early forties enjoy contemporary Christian music. Other styles of music should be used with other age groups.

You might provide light snacks and/or offer them something to drink (coffee, hot chocolate, soft drinks, or tea). People seem to relax when they have something in their hands. But be sensitive to those who are concerned about weight control. For example, you can serve both sweets and fruit, or alternate them each week.

Encourage people to talk with one another by including others in your conversations with people. You can ask about their week, work, and kids. Casual conversation can serve a purpose in warming up people to more meaningful conversation.

OPENING. Gather people together, welcome everyone, and acknowledge any newcomers. Cover any group business, but avoid setting the tone of a business meeting. Simply say something like, "There are a couple of things that you may want to know about . . . ." Also, review the group guidelines at this time. In 12-Step groups, the facilitator or someone else usually reads the 12 Steps at this point.

SHARING. Group members will benefit if people have a chance to tell what's going on in their lives. This allows for people to begin to get to know one another. It also provides an opportunity for a person to feel he is known by others as he talks about his life.

In the early stages of a group's growth, you should provide some additional guidance besides, "How are things going with you all?" When people first join a group, they are often hesitant to tell others much about themselves. They may not trust the group members yet or simply may not know how much disclosure is expected.

For the first few weeks you might begin by asking questions similar to the following:

"Tell us where you're from."

"Tell us where you work and what kind of work you do."

"Tell us how you met your wife (or husband)."

"Tell us the two best things your family did when you were growing up."

Later, as the members of the group have grown in their trust for one another, you can ask questions like, "What was the high point and the low point of your week?"

Be sure to affirm people's contributions, and avoid sarcastic or critical remarks like the plague!

PRAYER. A simple opening prayer by you or someone else in the group is appropriate for a group of Christians. Later, when the members know and feel comfortable with one another, you can spend more time praying for group requests.

DISCUSSION. The bulk of your group time will be spent in discussion of the topic for the week. The flow of the discussion can be traced through the following steps.

• ***Hook***. Begin the topic for the evening by raising their interest in the discussion. In this "hook" you are usually setting up some sort of tension, not between group members, but between competing ideas or concepts (*which is true?*) or between a good idea and its application (*is it practical?*). This tension propels the group's discussion forward.

For example, to "hook" a group into a discussion of God's love you must first narrow the topic. What about God's love do you wish to explore? Let us say you choose to focus upon the enduring character of God's love even when we sin. You can "hook" their interest in the discussion by explaining a hypothetical story of a young Christian girl who has gotten an abortion. She is concerned that God does not love her anymore.

Then ask, "What would you say to this girl about God's love?" Many Christians in your group might say something like, "Of course, God still loves you." If you leave the issue there, the discussion pretty much ends.

But if you say something like, "But what if the girl tells you, 'You don't understand! I told God to go to hell! I was going to do what I wanted and what He thought didn't matter.'" Some in your group will be stumped; they will be "hooked" into the discussion as they seek an answer to your question.

Others will attempt to resolve the tension by responding with something like, "Of course, God still loves you, if you say you're sorry." Tension resolves and the discussion faces a premature close. Again, add more information about this girl by saying, "But this girl doesn't want to say, 'Sorry.' She still believes she was right, and God was wrong. But she wants God's love. What would you say to her then?" You've reintroduced tension around the issue, "Is there a practical limit to God's love?" and still others are "hooked" into the discussion.

• ***Investigation.*** After you have raised the group's interest in the topic for the week, you will guide the group's discovery of the issues through your discussion questions. The key word here is "guide."

Consider the role of a trail guide for a horseback trip in the mountains. He knows where to go and how to get there, but he involves the tour group in the process of setting up camp, packing the horses, and preparing the meals. He knows when the trail opens into a beautiful valley and allows the group to precede him into the meadow. As a result, the people on the trip feel a sense of discovery and awe.

Your role as a guide is similar. You know where the group members need to go in their understanding and development, yet they need to discover these goals themselves. Your major tools are not horses and campsites, but good discussion questions. With them, you guide your group down the path of discovery.

On the practical side, if you are not using a study guide, you will need, first, to construct an outline of the topic and, second, to develop a series of good discussion questions. This takes a fair amount of experience to do well. If, on the other hand, you are using a study guide, such as one of Rapha's *Small Group Leader's Guides* which corresponds to our books, much of this work is already done for you. Even so, you may still need to come up with a few additional discussion questions to guide the discussion on asking good questions.

• ***Application.*** Ultimately, the tension over competing ideas (in our example, God's limited love vs. God's boundless love) probably will be resolved. You should, however, reintroduce the tension and keep the discussion going by focusing upon their application of the prevailing idea.

You can ask, "In what situations do you feel God withholds a portion of His love from you?" In this way, you focus the group's attention upon the application of the truth or insight into their lives.

Applications can be cognitive (what a person thinks), affective (what a person feels), or behavioral (what a person does). No single application fits every person. Rather, each group member should select applications which are appropriate for his or her own situation.

Many group leaders feel that the resolution of tension is necessary by the end of the meeting. Experienced leaders, however, know that unresolved tension will stimulate further reflection and discussion after the meeting is over. This provides an excellent beginning point for the next group meeting.

CLOSING. You should signal the end of the discussion and close the meeting. If the discussion has led to some resolution of the issues, you can simply say, "That about covers it for this evening. Let's close in prayer."

If, however, the group is still resolving the tension between ideas when closing time arrives, it is best to recap what conclusion(s) you have reached so far. You can say, "This has been profitable. I think we've made some progress. We've seen that . . . yet, we still need to resolve a couple of issues. So, we'll pick up here when we get back together next week."

If there are some business items which you would like people to remember, such as a social function or a change of meeting location for the next week, mention them at this time. However, avoid returning to a discussion of business items unless the group members strongly feel they would like to do so.

Be sure to end on time. Allow people, however, to stay and enjoy each other's company if they wish. This way, those who need to leave can do so without requiring everyone to discontinue their conversations, some of which can be more enriching than the group discussion itself.

SUGGESTED FORMAT FOR THE FIRST MEETING

SET YOUR OBJECTIVES

What do you want them to know?

- the purpose, format, and content of the group

What do you want them to feel?

- upbeat, safe, accepted, optimistic

What do you want them to do?

- make the group a part of their schedule, prepare for next week

MIXING

Set out a light snack and drinks; have some soft music playing in the background; create a warm and inviting atmosphere.

OPENING

• ***Welcome***

After you gather everyone together say, **"I'd like to welcome you all here this evening. I'm looking forward to getting to know you, and I hope and pray that you will benefit from our times together. Even though some of us know one another, why don't we begin by going around the room and introducing ourselves?"** At this point you are covering the basic question, *Who are these people?*

• ***Purpose and ground rules***

Clarify the group's expectations by stating the purpose of the group and discussing ground rules. (See Chapter 4.) You are answering the unasked question, *Why am I here?*

One way you can proceed is by saying the following:

"I know I've talked with each of you a little bit about the direction this group will take. We're here to . . . . " (In one simple sentence, write out the purpose of the group.)

"As we pursue this purpose, I think it will be helpful if we discuss a few simple ground rules and expectations we will have of one another.

"For example, a couple of ground rules I'd like to suggest are, first, that we not repeat outside of the group the things we hear in the group. Maintain confidentiality by letting people tell their own stories."

"Second, that we allow others the chance to express what they think and feel, but that we do not force one another to talk if they do not wish to.

"What other ground rules do you think we ought to follow?" The group members may be reluctant to contribute. So you may need to construct the list yourself. Conclude with, **"Good. I think this gives us a starting place. We'll return to this list from time to time and add to or modify it as needed."**

SHARING

After the basic introductions, introduce yourself by sharing your background and interest in the group. Continue with the sharing by saying something like, **"I'd like us to get to know one another a little bit better. I'd like to go around the room again and have everyone tell us also where you're from and what kind of work you do."**

PRAYER

Lead the group in a brief prayer; focus on thanks to God for His character and His concerns for us.

DISCUSSION

(Raise interest in the group by leading a brief discussion on the reasons why the topic will benefit the members. You can then briefly discuss some of the questions in the first lesson if time permits. Remember, the primary goal of the first meeting is for people to feel welcome and safe, not to "get through the material.")

- **Hook** (What launching question will you use?)

- **Investigation** (What central issue will be covered in the group over the next several weeks?)

- **Application** (List possible cognitive, affective, and behavioral applications.)
  - Survey the ground rules, format, and content for the group; encourage and answer questions from the group.
  - Be sure everyone has materials.

CLOSING

- Review any business items members need to remember.

WEEKLY CHECKLIST

SIX DAYS BEFORE THE GROUP MEETS

- Prepare the flow of the meeting and discussion
- Collect any special materials needed for the group
- Pray for the group members

THREE DAYS BEFORE THE GROUP MEETS

- Confirm the location
- Call anyone who missed last week
- Prepare any snacks

DAY OF THE MEETING

- Set up signs for directions, if needed
- Set up the chairs in the room
- Set out the snacks
- Check the temperature and lighting
- Turn on the music
- Pray with your co-leader, if you have one.

MEETING FORMAT WORKSHEET

OBJECTIVES

What do you want them to know?

What do you want them to feel?

What do you want them to do?

MIXING

OPENING

SHARING

(What will you ask them to share about?)

PRAYER

(If so, who and how long?)

DISCUSSION

- Hook (What launching question will you use?)

- Investigation (Which ideas will be held in tension during the group?)

- Application (List possible cognitive, affective, and behavioral applications.)

CLOSING

Asking Good Questions

Your group discussions live or die based upon the questions you ask. Any question you ask will be leading, closed, or open. A ***leading question*** ("You agree that God loves you, don't you?") is rhetorical, not discussion-generating. It expects the person to agree. Trial attorneys use this kind of question to force the person giving testimony into a direction in which the attorney wishes to go. The answer is strongly implied in its asking. It may be effective when used appropriately; nevertheless, use it infrequently.

The ***limiting question*** takes the form of a guessing game. Kids sometimes play the game "Stick Quiz." One child says to another, "I'm thinking of a number between one and ten. What is it?" If the second child guesses wrong, he gets slapped on the back of the hand with a stick or ruler.

You can play the same game with your group by asking questions like, "What two ways can we accomplish this task?" or "What is the main emotion the author expresses here?" If the members guess wrong, you send the non-verbal message, *Wrong! Boy, are you out of it.* People keep guessing until they hit upon the answer you have in mind or, more than likely, they'll quit trying to answer. "Stick Quiz" is a discussion killer. Avoid playing the game while you are leading others to discover the truth.

Limiting questions sometimes resemble exams more than a guessing game. The leader asks a question which tests the knowledge of the participants. For example, while discussing anger in a grief support group a leader may ask, "What three things did Jesus say to His disciples about anger?" Group members are expected to fill in the blank with the correct answer. Grade schoolers sometimes enjoy succeeding at fill-in-the-blank, but adolescents and adults usually do not like to participate when these types of questions are used.

However, for all their weaknesses, limiting questions and, to a lesser degree, leading questions, can play a useful role in a group discussion. For example, by using limiting questions you can help people discover the content of a passage of Scripture. As you teach Titus 2:3–9, for example, you can say, "Notice that in verses four, eight, and ten, Paul includes the clause 'so that . . .' at the end of each verse. What concern does he reflect in these clauses?" This limiting question causes the group to reflect and synthesize an answer. Notice, however, you should follow this limiting question with an open question such as, "What are some examples of what can happen if we do not reflect a similar concern in our conduct?"

The best way to stimulate discussion is to ask ***open questions***. They focus upon who, what, when, where, how, and why; but the answers are not limited to a specific set of data. For example, "Why do you think Paul said, 'Flee immorality' to his readers?" is an open question. With an open question, people's input is valued and their minds are engaged in thinking about the issue at hand. They are not guessing at what answer you are looking for. You communicate that you value their input.

Open questions are frequently begun with phrases like, "In what ways . . ." "Why do you think . . ." "How does one . . ." and "Who do you suppose . . . ." Even the person with little biblical knowledge can become the expert when you ask, "In your opinion . . . ?"

Often group members will ask you to give the correct answer to questions they have. If you answer them directly, you will rob them of the joy of discovering the answer for themselves. You can handle the situation by asking them the question, "What would you say?" or "What do you think?" (These are return questions.) Or you can allow others to give their input by asking, "What do the rest of you think?" (Here, you are using a relay question.)

Evaluation Questions

1. Why is it important to have objectives in all three areas: know, feel, and do?

2. Describe the meeting format which seems most appropriate for your style of leadership and your group:

3. Indicate whether the following questions are **leading**, **limiting**, or **open**.

   - What does God say about anger?
   - How often did Jesus say we should forgive people who have harmed us?
   - Don't you think we should "get it off our chest" when we're angry?
   - What does 1 Corinthians 13:10 say? Who can quote that?
   - How do you feel when Jesus says, "You cannot serve God and money"?

   Rephrase the leading and limiting questions above and make them open questions.

4. How would you explain the difference between a group which uses open questions and one that allows any answer, biblical or not, to stand unchallenged?

Setting the Environment

OBJECTIVES

- to examine important practical environmental elements which can promote effective communication in the group, and
- to determine ground rules for your group environment.

PART OF YOUR ROLE as a leader is to set the stage for God to work in people's lives. Attention given to the seemingly unexciting details of a group meeting will provide a better environment in which God can work.

Meeting Site

Select a site for your meeting that is comfortable and accessible. If your small group functions as part of a larger group format (for example, Sunday School program, women's ministry program, or men's prayer breakfast), the meeting place for your group may already be determined. In this case, you may have little control over the comfort of the room.

On the other hand, you may have more freedom to select the site for your group. A home environment can be a good choice. Many people enjoy the comforts of a living room environment for their church-sponsored small groups. If you meet in your home or in the home of a group member, consider the following:

- Keep distractions to a minimum; children should be reliably in bed or with a sitter, pets should be restricted, phone calls should be answered by a machine, and the front door should be answered quietly.

- Provide comfortable seating; couches and chairs should be arranged so that everyone can see the others in the group, avoid over-crowding.

- Minimize entertaining; fancy refreshments, decorations, or dress tend to put people on their social best, they are not free to be themselves during the group interaction; some may perceive the host as wanting to "show off" his or her home and become resentful.

- Make an appropriate room selection; the living room or den is usually best; some climates may allow comfortable use of the patio, but distractions are greater outdoors (wildlife, plane overflights, insects, etc.); do not use a pool-side patio.

Seating Arrangement

Arrange the seating so that each person can see every other person in the group. A circle works best. In addition, place your chair so that it is on the same level as the rest of the group—neither at the focal point of the group nor in the background.

Be especially sensitive to the seating arrangement in

groups such as sexual abuse recovery groups. Some people feel "trapped" if there is not at least one opening between the chairs in the group. Others may feel exposed and vulnerable if anyone is behind them. In these groups, ask how people feel about the seating arrangement, and strive to promote an emotionally safe environment. Be aware that the further apart people sit, the less likely they will be to share their thoughts and feelings. Large rooms may be excellent for large groups, but they are killers of discussion unless the seating is placed relatively close together. For example, circle the chairs together in a large classroom, and move the furniture in a living room. This may take a little extra work, but the benefits will be significant.

Child Care

If your group members have small children, be sensitive to their ability to obtain reasonably priced child care as you select your group time and location. Some churches encourage the growth of their small group ministries by providing inexpensive or free child care one night a week. Members simply leave their children at the church and proceed to the location of their small group. Other situations will require members to obtain their own child care. In these cases, you might help by gathering a list of reliable and reasonably priced sitters for your group.

Outside Contact

In growth groups you may wish to contact everyone by phone or in person for the first two or three weeks your group meets to remind them of the meeting. Once the group has met consistently for three or so weeks, you can assume everyone has it on their calendars. They probably do not need a reminder.

Encourage members of the group to contact anyone who misses the meetings. If the leader contacts them, they may think, *Yeah, you're supposed to call me; you want your group to succeed.* But out of genuine concern, if another member contacts the person who missed, the person will likely think, *You know, these people care about me.*

In addition, establish a rapport with each group member or married couple outside the group meeting. This strengthens your relationships with the members by building trust and demonstrating that you care about them. Finally, encourage members to get to know one another through holiday parties and other social events. This provides a way for members to develop deep relationships.

The confidential nature of support groups, however, generally makes it inappropriate for the facilitator to pursue new members to remind them of the meeting. These people may feel pressured and controlled by these calls. The facilitator may, however, ask if anyone would like to be called to be reminded of the group. Outside activities, such as informal parties, can be offered after the group has been meeting for a while.

In both growth and support groups, encourage responsible, healthy relationships outside the group meetings. Be aware, however, that the temptation toward cliques or sexual affairs may occur if the level of emotional intensity in the group heightens. This will ultimately devastate the individuals and their families, as well as the group. It may be very helpful to group members for you to lead a discussion on the possibilities and liabilities of an absorbing and exclusive relationship.

Homework

To get the most out of the group experience, people can be encouraged to reflect on the concepts between meetings. Homework is a good way to help a group member keep working on group issues. Rapha books have either a workbook or reflection/discussion questions at the end of the chapters for that purpose. Many of the books also include a group leader's guide with suggested questions which will help group members focus on central concerns.

Be sure everyone has access to the materials with which they are to complete their homework.

Non-verbal Communication

Communicate love, acceptance, and warmth non-verbally. For example, if you rarely smile, people will think (often subconsciously) that you do not appreciate them. Additionally, if you have a habit of furrowing your brow when you listen to someone's question, you may need to learn new nonverbal communication. You may actually be thinking about what someone is saying, but it signals displeasure to many people. Likewise, avoid crossing your arms when listening to people. That gesture often communicates a defensive or resistant attitude.

You can also communicate love by appropriate touch. Shake everyone's hand; this is appropriate for both men and women. Be sensitive, however, to people who simply do not want to be touched. You will only increase their feelings of resentment if you attempt to force them to accept touch. Be sure to follow commonly accepted social norms for touch.

The Size of Your Group

Discussions are best conducted in groups of about eight to ten people. In groups larger than twelve participants, people do not have enough time to talk and involve themselves in the discussion. On the other hand, group sizes of five people or less can produce low quality discussions.

When inviting people to join your group, keep in mind

your ideal group size. If 12 people, for example, say they will come to your group, usually you will have six to ten people attend your group each week. However, if you receive commitments from eight people to participate in the group, you may have weeks where only four people show up and your discussion may suffer as a result.

Your group may prosper and swell to over 12 people in size. You can provide people with a greater chance to participate in the discussion by breaking the larger group into two sub-groups during portions of your discussion. Give each of the smaller groups the same question or issue to discuss. After ten to twenty minutes, pull the sub-groups back into one larger group and ask people to share what they learned in the smaller groups. If attendance continues to remain large, consider appointing or recruiting another leader and offering two separate groups.

Open and Closed Groups

Closed groups limit membership once the group has started. This allows trust to build and relationships to develop without constantly "backtracking" when new members join the group. The weakness is that the group can become inwardly focused and even cliquish. This tends to limit the amount of church growth which can take place through groups.

Open groups, however, welcome new members at any time during the course of the group. This allows the group to grow. In addition, the numbers of groups will multiply if groups separate into smaller groups when they become too large. Open groups tend to experience less emotional openness and intensity than closed groups.

In some cases, you may wish to close your group even if it began as an open group. For example, one woman led a group for three months. During the fourth month, the members began being more open and honest with one another. Then a new member began attending who disrupted the open and safe atmosphere with her domineering behavior. When the new member was present, the older members were silent, but in her absence, they talked freely of their struggles. The leader met with the new member and gently directed her to another group, saying, "We appreciate your coming to our group, but I feel that another group might be better suited for you." If you face such a situation and must close your group, help the new member understand that the issue is one of familiarity and stages of personal growth, not one of rejection or acceptance.

Recruiting a Co-leader

Co-leading helps in three ways. First, a co-leader can assist you in the running of the group. He or she can substitute for you should you become ill, help manage the details of the group business, or handle portions of the group meeting itself. Having someone to share the burdens of the group helps increase your ability to lead groups for more than a season.

Second, a co-leader can detect when you get drawn into the emotion of a meeting and lose your objectivity and effectiveness. For example, a group member may criticize your leadership or a particular point you make in a discussion. You may be hurt and become angry. You may even become vulnerable to the temptation to take revenge in some subtle form (such as through sarcasm). A trusted co-leader can give you feedback concerning your reactions to the group members and your overall effectiveness as a leader. Part of this feedback process involves your ability to "blow off steam" with a trusted co-leader concerning the people or situations in your group.

Third, a person with limited leadership experience can gain a wealth of insight and skills by co-leading a group under a qualified leader or facilitator. This method of grooming co-leaders to be competent leaders is one of the most effective methods of training.

The major guidelines for selecting a co-leader or co-facilitator are a mutual respect and an open line of communication. It is doubtful, and even undesirable, that the co-leaders agree on everything said and done in the group. Differences in personality, approach, and experience add to the richness of co-leading. Unless the leaders and co-leaders respect one another, however, these differences will erupt into conflict and will negatively influence the effectiveness of the group. Likewise, unless time is allotted for talking together about the direction of the group, confusion, frustration, and misdirection can occur in the group meetings.

Ground Rules

Every group establishes norms consisting of appropriate behaviors for members. This process often occurs subconsciously without discussion. However, your group will benefit if you discuss any group goals, formatting, and expectations at the first meeting and review them from time to time. This allows the group to participate in the formulation of the group's ground rules. This takes the spotlight off of you and gives the members a sense of ownership in the group.

GROWTH GROUP GROUND RULES

- We encourage you to share as little or as much of your experience as you wish.
- Allow others the chance to express what they think and feel. However, do not force others to talk if they do not wish to.
- We all deal with life in different ways. Avoid passing judgment on others and give advice only with permission.
- Do not repeat outside of the group the things you hear within the group. Maintain confidentiality by letting people tell their own stories. The only exception is when someone's safety or property is in danger.
- Give a good effort to prepare the lessons for each week.
- Pray for and welcome new members.
- Enjoy the relationships you develop here.

SUPPORT GROUP GROUND RULES

- "Everything we say in here stays in here."
- Use "I" statements, not "you" statements.
- Don't use humor to cover your pain.
- You don't have to say anything if you don't want to.
- Don't "fix" people's problems and feelings.
- Don't give advice unless it is requested.

Evaluation Questions

1. What are your plans for "setting the environment" for your group?

   Meeting site -

   Seating arrangement -

   Childcare -

   Outside contact -

   Homework -

   Size of the group -

   Open or closed group -

   A co-leader -

2. Why are ground rules important? What are some potential problems if each of these ground rules are not followed?

3. What specific ground rules will you need for your group? How, when, and how often will you communicate them?

The Dynamics of a Group

OBJECTIVES

- to give an understanding of the elements which provide safety, trust, and encouragment for group members,
- to examine the character and skills of an effective group leader, and
- to provide an overview of the stages of a group.

KNOWING THE REASONS WHY some groups progress while others do poorly will help you gain more control over the course of your group. You will be able to detect potential problems and understand what will be needed in order to enhance the effectiveness of your group.

Group dynamics refers to the life and growth of the group and of the individuals who attend. The stages of interaction between members over time are affected by the group environment and the character and skills of the group leader. The following material is drawn from a combined experience of over forty years in leading small groups. Even so, we also draw upon the insights of others, especially Corey and Corey (*Groups: Process and Practice*, 3d ed., Pacific Grove, CA: Brooks/Cole, 1987).

Group dynamics will be explored as we examine several essential ingredients:

- elements of an effective group environment,
- dynamics of leadership,
- stages of development of a group leader, and
- stages of a group.

Elements of an Effective Group Environment

Several key elements contribute significantly to an environment in which God can change lives. Any of these elements alone can stimulate growth in people. Each element, however, contributes to the effectiveness of the other elements. Thus, the combination of these elements in your group is a powerful tool in God's hands.

LOVE AND ACCEPTANCE

As the leader, if you regularly display love and acceptance in the group, you will provide a safe environment for change. People need to know that others care for them. On the positive side, you display that love by accepting people regardless of where they are in their spiritual life. By showing interest in people, listening to their ideas and concerns, appreciating their contributions and affirming their value, you can show others that you accept them.

If, however, you frequently correct people's ideas, ridicule the opinions of others who are not members of the group, frown a lot, make sarcastic jokes, or even wait for others to initiate conversations with you, you communicate a lack of acceptance. You may genuinely love people, but unless you communicate that love verbally and non-verbally, others may not perceive your love. To accept someone does not mean you approve of everything that person does. For example, God accepts His children because of what Christ has done, yet He does not approve of all that His children choose to do. He loves and accepts us as His children even though we still sin.

SAFETY AND TRUST

Provide a safe place. Significant change in patterns of living and thinking is risky. People need a safe place in which to think about the changes God wants them to make in their lives. They need to feel secure in order to consider serious changes in long-term patterns of relating to God and others. Therefore, you need to develop an atmosphere of trust and stability. Your loving and accepting people without precondition contributes significantly to their personal security. If people know they will not be rejected for what they say or do, they will feel safe in your acceptance. Yet, you can further build a secure atmosphere in your group through maintaining confidentiality and consistency.

Confidentiality. After a measure of trust has developed in an atmosphere of unconditional love, members will begin to reveal sensitive facets of their lives to the group. If a member shares this information with someone who is not a member of the group, confidentiality is then broken and mutual trust may be seriously handicapped.

Sometimes members of the group will ask you, as the leader, for advice on private matters. If you later mention what you know of their situation to the group, you will have signalled to the rest of the group your inability to keep information in confidence. You also seriously erode the trust these people placed in you when they sought your advice.

Perhaps the most common way in which confidentiality is breached in Christian circles is through the sharing of "prayer requests." What begins as well-intentioned concern often turns into a non-vicious form of gossip which is, nonetheless, hurtful. This often occurs when people wish to "pray specifically" for a person's needs and they inquire about the details of the situation. As they share this "prayer concern" to others, they convert private matters into public knowledge. Confidentiality is lost and the safe environment of the group is compromised. A simple rule for maintaining confidence is, "Let people tell their own stories," or said another way, "Tell your own story, not someone else's." By following this maxim, you will avoid betraying others' confidence.

The only exception to this position on confidentiality is when someone volunteers information that reveals a danger, actual or threatened, to someone's safety or property. In most states, people who are aware of these threats must report them to the proper authorities. For example, if someone reveals a situation where child abuse is occurring, the group leader, and other members as well, must report this knowledge to the state's Child Protective Services. Or, if a man says, "I'm so mad at my company for firing me, I'm going to burn it down. And I know just how to do it, too." Many times, people say drastic things without any intention of following through with them. Exercise discernment. Ask a few questions, and if you believe the threat is real, report this threat to the police. Someone may mention his desire to end his own life. This, too, is an exception to the principle of confidentiality.

In light of these possibilities, you may wish to mention this exception in one of your first group meetings. For example, you can read the statement of confidentiality and then add, "The only exceptions are any mention of a danger to someone's safety or property. In these cases, everyone in the group is bound by law to report these situations to the proper authorities."

Consistency. People, on the whole, unconsciously look for patterns of reliability before they place their trust in others. Your consistency will contribute to group members' ability to trust both you and the rest of the group.

Consistency is reflected in a variety of tangible ways. For example, starting and ending your group on time, meeting at the same place and time each week, and following the same meeting format communicate consistency. Less tangible actions also affect the overall impression of consistency. The group leader who is sporadically available for conversation outside the group or who displays periodic rejection of other's opinions will experience difficulty establishing an atmosphere of consistency. Absolute consistency is not possible or, perhaps, even desirable. You can, however, strive for an overall pattern of reliability in what you say and do.

EMPATHY AND COMFORT

Most people want to be understood, especially if they are going through difficult times. Even when life's circumstances are fairly stable, knowing that someone else understands gives comfort. When you lend an empathetic ear you display a deep understanding of someone's situation. You are, in effect, saying, *You are not alone.* That comforts people. The Apostle Paul instructed the early church to "rejoice with those who rejoice, weep with those who weep," and speaks of God as the "God of all comfort" and the One "who comforts the downcast" (Romans 12:14; 2 Corinthians 1:3; 7:6). By modeling God's comforting character in your group, you provide God the opportunity to change lives.

Active listening plays a central role in empathy. We often listen to others while thinking about how we are going to respond. An active listener, on the other hand, is not primarily concerned with his own response. Rather, he focuses not only upon what a person is saying but upon the thoughts and feelings revealed by the speaker. This focus allows the listener to feel, in a limited way, the feelings of the one who is talking.

HOPE AND ENCOURAGEMENT

Comfort in the present leads to hope for the future and the encouragement we all need to go on. If people have reason to hope and their hopes are realistic, they can endure the process of change. The balance between admitting the scope of one's problems and developing a hope for change can be a delicate one. For example, you may notice the members of your group becoming gloomy and depressed as they realize the difficulties they face. You will need to encourage them without minimizing the difficult task before them.

POWER AND CONTROL

Many people have been victimized during their lives. The abuse may have been emotional, physical, or sexual, and may have occurred in childhood and adulthood alike. People, however, need to see themselves as more than victims. They need a sense of power and control over their own lives. Your group can help people grasp the fact that they do have choices, that they have the ability to gain control over the way they live.

To some Christians, this sounds like a concession to self-centeredness, however, the need for a sense of power and control over our lives does not necessarily run counter to a Christ-centered life. God enables us to make responsible choices. We can either choose to follow His leadership and make healthy (but often hard) choices about our behaviors, relationships, and feelings, or we can acquiesce to others' manipulation. The ability to make good choices is based in a sense of personal power and control in our lives.

God provides people the power they need to change. For example, Paul wrote Timothy, "For God has not given us a spirit of timidity, but a spirit of power, of love, and of self-discipline" (2 Timothy 1:7). Elsewhere, he prays for his readers that God "may strengthen you with power through His Spirit in your inner being" (Ephesians 3:16). God wishes through His Spirit and His power to strengthen and empower us at the core of who we are. God does not oppose personal power and control. He opposes misused personal power and control, a personal power and control used in rebellion against Him. You can encourage your group, "Through God's strength, you have the power and ability to change."

OPENNESS AND HONESTY

People are more likely to change when they perceive the need to do so, but people are often reluctant to acknowledge their needs. By fostering open and honest group interaction, you model for people the honesty required to admit a need to change.

We can be honest in a couple of ways. First, we can be honest with ourselves about ourselves; this requires vulnerability. If you, for example, can admit to yourself that you are at times fearful, you have made the first step toward change. In addition, if you can admit your fear to the group, you are telling the group, *It's okay to admit your fears.*

Second, we can be honest with others about how we perceive or feel about them; this requires love. "Brutal honesty," however, should not be allowed. Paul instructed his readers to speak "the truth in love" (Ephesians 4:15). When a person is honest about how he or she feels about or perceives another, he or she should focus upon the well-being of that other person.

FREEDOM OF EXPRESSION

Give people the freedom to express their thoughts and feelings, hopes and dreams, and fears and failures. Not everyone will share these things with the group to the same degree or depth, especially in the early stages of your group, but you can provide the freedom for them to do so if they wish. As you plan for each session, prepare opportunities for people to talk, feel, and act during the group. Give people the opportunity to sample new ideas, perspectives, and feelings. This includes the use of open-ended and feeling-oriented questions, a relaxed atmosphere, a non-judgmental attitude, and even silence.

When people experience love and acceptance, they will often express how they really feel about the situations in their lives. They may even express pent-up feelings in powerful ways by bursting into sobs, shaking uncontrollably, or speaking quite harshly about others who have harmed them. This emotional release can be a healthy way for people to face the truth about how they really feel. Isolated emotional release, however, carries little long-term benefit. They need to understand the cause of those powerful feelings, grieve their wounds, experience love and grace, and learn to forgive those who have hurt them.

INFORMATION AND PERSPECTIVE

People need to know what to think and do when they encounter new difficulties in life. Even in the absence of stress, people want and need to learn how to grow in their walk with God and in their relationships with family, friends, and co-workers. Remember to include factual information in your weekly meetings about the topic that has brought the group members together. Discussion which focuses on causes, symptoms, and remedies for the difficulties and challenges of life is a necessary part of any successful group.

Emotional release alone is not sufficient to produce long-term benefits and changes. People need to couple this release with a new perspective, a new way of looking at things, so they can learn to interpret their emotions and responses to hurtful situations. The information you provide (not by a lecture, but through a discussion format) can assist the group members in putting their emotional experience into words. In this way, they can gain the perspective they need in order to make responsible changes in their responses to people.

Each of these elements may not be present in your group each time it meets. For example, you may spend most of your time one week comforting people who have encountered particularly difficult situations. As a result, you will be high in comfort and low in information (because you ran out of time). You can, however, strive for an overall balance between the elements.

In addition, you will find that you will have strengths which cause you to emphasize a certain element or two. For example, your group's strengths may be freedom of expression and honesty, and yet, the content occasionally may be deficient. Be grateful for your strengths and devote a little extra effort to improving the other areas.

Dynamics of Leadership

You could probably fill yards of shelf space with recent books which discuss the essential characteristics and skills of leadership in general and group leadership in particular. Our discussion will not replace these books, but will focus upon the essential elements you will need for leading your small group.

THE CHARACTER OF THE LEADER

The essential element in the effectiveness of your group is you. Your content, skills, techniques, preparation, and ideas are all important. Yet, who you are, not just what you do, is the common denominator. Time spent on development of your character will yield the most benefit for your group. In his recent book, *How to Get Along with Almost Anyone*, H. Norman Wright notes the three basic qualities needed to get along well with a variety of people. These same qualities, genuineness, nonpossessive love, and empathy, also play a key role in your effectiveness as a group leader.

Genuineness. To be an effective group leader or facilitator you must be genuine. The apostle Paul insisted that church leaders possess this quality, and he displayed it in his dealings with the churches (1 Timothy 3:8; 2 Corinthians 1:12). Genuine people encourage trust, and people feel safe with a genuine group leader. Synonyms of "genuine" are: authentic, bona fide, original, valid, veritable, guileless, natural, sincere, unaffected, and unfeigned. When you are genuine no one has to read between the lines, no one has to interpret you, no one has to wonder if you are really what you say you are. Genuine people do not wear masks or put on fronts. They are real.

Transparency and openness are related to genuineness. Being open and transparent does not mean you "spill your guts" to everyone you meet. Something is wrong with the person who shares his most personal failures with a cab driver. Transparency means being seen for who you really are, not by everyone, but to those with whom you share a personal relationship. It involves honesty and integrity; what you are in public (in the eyes of others) is what you are in private.

Nonpossessive love. The second essential quality possessed by an effective group leader is a nonpossessive love. Loving others is second only to loving God and is the mark of authentic Christianity (Matthew 22:37–39; John 13:35, 17:23; 1 John 4:7–8; 20). Many people confuse love with sentimentality or emotions. However, the biblical authors focus upon the action of love, not its emotions. Sentiment and emotion may accompany love, but its essence is action. For example, Jesus was not sentimental or warmly emotional as He hung on the cross, yet He conclusively displayed God's love. Loving actions include: caring, kindness, gentleness, respect, fairness, and even rebuke, which come from a motivation to build and not destroy the person.

Nonpossessive love distinguishes between the person and the deeds. For example, Jesus displayed nonpossessive love in His encounter with a rich young man. Though He loved the man, He allowed him to walk away from eternal life (Mark 10:17–23). Love does not blur the boundaries between individuals but allows others to express their own individuality, even if their choices are wrong. We can disapprove of and even limit people's misbehavior and still love them.

Empathy. Empathy is defined as the "identification with and understanding of another's situation, feelings, and motives" (*The New American Heritage Dictionary*). It involves seeing another's world through his or her eyes, and gives others the great sense they are understood. Norm Wright distinguishes between empathy, sympathy, and apathy. He observes, "Apathy has no feelings, sympathy is feeling for another; and empathy is feeling with another. Apathy says, *I don't care*; sympathy says, *Oh, you poor thing*; and empathy says, *It looks like you're having a difficult time today.*" People do not want our sympathy, much less our apathy; they want our empathy.

It should be obvious that many thousands of work-related meetings are conducted each day, very few of which are characterized by the qualities we have described. Task-oriented groups can function without genuineness, nonpossessive love, and empathy, yet people will not grow in their personal and spiritual lives without these elements being present in their leaders.

THE BASIC SKILLS OF THE LEADER

Character deals with who we are; skill determines what we do. Those who possess more character qualities will reap the greatest results from developing their skills. Some of these skills include:

Active listening. The active listener is one who is alert to all the levels of communication being used by a speaker. When people speak up in a small group (or anywhere else), they use more than words to communicate with others. They use changes in tone of voice, body posture, facial expressions, and word choices to communicate their thoughts and feelings. Active listeners are alert to these signals and the messages they communicate.

Sometimes people send conflicting messages. For example, a man may be talking about the peace of God in his life and yet display considerable agitation through his harsh tone of voice and clinched fists. Or, a young woman may say, "I hate my mother for not shielding me from my father. But she's such a weak person and I love her." Group leaders need to pay particularly close attention because conflicting messages are often separated by several minutes, sometimes even days or weeks.

You can increase your active listening skills by becoming aware of the factors, both external and internal, which cause you to give too little attention to what other people are saying. External distractions can usually be corrected easily, such as when loud noises occur in the adjoining room or hallway. Internal distractions require more awareness and effort to overcome. For example, you may be upset because you quarreled with your spouse just before leaving home for the group meeting. As a result, you will likely not be able to listen as attentively as you otherwise might. In this situation, the distraction is temporary, unless, of course, you quarrel frequently. Other distractions are more pervasive, such as when a leader fears failure and rejection if group members disagree with him. Group leaders must work harder to surmount these barriers to active listening.

Encouraging openness. Leaders who learn to draw people out and involve them in the group will increase their group's cohesiveness and, hence, their effectiveness as a leader. Encouraging people to share themselves includes asking people about themselves, what they think, what they feel, what their family is like, and what their interests and hobbies are. It also entails valuing and affirming them and, conversely, avoiding personal attacks and criticisms. By doing this, you communicate, *You matter to me and to this group. You can make a contribution.*

Drawing people out pivots on the attitude of the leader toward the group members. Leaders who view members as "lost sheep" in desperate need of direction will have a difficult time involving people in the group. Group members will likely assume the role of passive receivers of information and control. On the other hand, leaders who hold people in high regard will make ample room for the contributions of group members. Members become actively involved in the group and contribute to others.

Facilitating. The difference between encouraging openness and facilitating is one of focus. Drawing people out focuses on urging individuals to share themselves with others. Facilitating focuses upon the dynamics of the group when people begin to communicate and contribute. One precedes the other, but both are closely linked. Corey and Corey, in *Groups: Process and Practice*, lists ways leaders can facilitate group interaction. They can: 1) assist members to express honestly their fears and expectations; 2) work to create an atmosphere of safety and acceptance; 3) encourage and support members as they explore new ideas and behaviors; 4) involve as many people as possible in the interaction; 5) work to lessen dependency upon the group leader; 6) encourage open expression of conflict and controversy; and 7) help members remove hindrances to direct communication. In short, cultivate open and responsible communication.

Knowing limits. You will likely face situations which exceed your ability to handle effectively. Indeed, very few professionals can deal with every type of problem people face. You will need to: 1) seek outside advice for yourself as you deal with group situations, or 2) refer a group member to a more qualified resource. By knowing your limits, you can avoid a lot of grief for yourself and for your group members.

For example, someone in your group may say, "I've given this some thought and I'm leaving my wife." Unless you have training and experience in marriage counseling, you should refer this person to your pastor or a Christian marriage and family counselor in your area. Likewise, if someone volunteers, "I don't feel like life is worth living," "I've recently had flashbacks of my father visiting my bedroom late at night," or "I sometimes hear voices and can't find who's speaking," you should suggest that person talk with a Christian professional counselor.

Stages of Development of a Group Leader

Group leaders go through stages as they develop in their leadership skills. They may spend anywhere from a few minutes to a few weeks or months in each stage. Training, experience, and feedback from more experienced leaders can help you move through these stages.

STAGE ONE: FOCUS ON SELF

Inexperienced leaders usually fear the prospect of failing in their groups. Consequently, they tend to center upon how they will be perceived and focus mostly upon their performance. They may ask themselves questions like, *How am I doing?* or *Do these people like me?* During the group discussion, leaders in this stage will be anxious. They will likely talk too much, speak rapidly, feel uncomfortable with silence, or fail to listen actively to the members' comments (because they are thinking about what they are going to say next). As a result, the members will not feel relaxed and secure, and they will take fewer risks in talking about the real issues of life.

STAGE TWO: FOCUS ON CONTENT

After leaders feel secure, they will shift their attention to the content of the group discussion. The accuracy, relevancy, and clarity of the content occupy their minds as they thoroughly prepare the "lesson." Questions which dominate their thoughts include, *Is this content any good? Is it worthwhile? Does it hold people's interest?*

A group led by a person in this content-oriented stage may display the following traits:

- too much reliance upon the group leader as he or she consults tightly worded and constructed notes;
- little room for other ideas in the discussion;
- too much focus upon ideas and too little expression of feelings and emotion;
- group discussion is minimal and the leader shifts to a lecture style of communication to fill the void; and
- focus is centered upon the leader and not upon the relationships and interaction of the group.

STAGE THREE: FOCUS ON PEOPLE

Competent leaders tend to focus upon the welfare of the group members. Areas of concern include: *How is the group interacting together? How is each member responding; how does he or she feel? Are the members growing as individuals and as a group?* The effective small group leader functions at this level on a regular basis.

THE "IDEAL" GROUP LEADER

This manual includes the insights of seasoned group leaders. We have selected the best advice available from a variety of sources. Yet, no one individual perfectly follows all the advice given or exhibits all the qualities and skills of an effective group leader. Each person possesses unique strengths and abilities which enable him or her to excel in one or two areas of group leadership. Very few people excel in every area. You may be overwhelmed with the thought of leading a group "by the manual." Take courage: God *can* and *will* use you if you seek to prepare to the best of your ability, trust Him throughout the process, and love your group members.

As you start your first group, remember, "Love covers a multitude of sins" (1 Peter 4:8). Many people stumble through the mechanics of a small group, clueless as to what they are trying to accomplish, yet they experience success because they love the members of the group. Even if you fail in your first few attempts at leading a group, God can use your experience to develop your leadership skills—if you keep going. Most successful leaders can tell stories of their own group failures. The only difference between you and them is the time it takes to learn from one's mistakes.

Stages of a Group

Each newly-formed group progresses through various stages as the members identify and bond with one another. Through understanding these stages you can gain insight into the responses you receive from the group. You will also understand how to meet the needs of group members during these stages.

STAGE ONE: EXPLORATION

As most people join a group, they are asking themselves (consciously or unconsciously) the following questions.

Who are these people?
Will I be in or out of this group?
If I join, how involved will I be?
Do I belong here; will they accept me?
Do these people like me; do I like them?
How much do I want to risk?
Can I really trust these people?
What's this group really about?
What's expected of me?
Do I fit and belong in here?
Can I be myself and be a part of this group?

In doing so, they are exploring the group and its possibilities. In this stage, people tend to give only basic information about themselves and accept others on a superficial level. They experience various levels of anxiety and are hesitant and insecure. Periods of awkward silence may occur in the group.

The group leader can best help the group members navigate the first stage by establishing trust through the creation of an atmosphere of security. People need to feel safe, especially if they are expected to talk about themselves in any fashion. You can develop their sense of security by doing the following.

Display a commitment to the group. By your commitment to preparation, punctuality, consistency, and enthusiasm you communicate that you are "in there" with the group members. Communicate expectations. Cover the ground rules weekly. Adhere to them consistently. Be sure to include the members in the formulation of the ground rules.

Take individual interest in the group members. Give attention to remembering people's names, dealing with their concerns, and appreciating their contributions. This affirms each member's value and creates security.

Deal positively with people's concerns. If you discount a member's concern over child care, for instance, you signal not only your insensitivity but your lack of commitment to them.

Respond properly to painful emotions. As members feel comfortable in the group, painful and profound emotions may surface. Someone may become angry or cry, for example. If you subtly try to scold them for their anger or display an awkwardness at their tears, you will effectively signal that people should control their emotions in the group. Their trust will be limited to the exchange of ideas and opinions, and your effectiveness as a leader will be limited.

Remember: your group members are depending on you. Your honesty, spontaneity, genuineness, and warmth communicates, *I am a safe person*, and people will trust your leadership.

STAGE TWO: TRANSITION

Typically, your group will go through a transition stage after the exploration phase. Positive elements of an effective group will begin to emerge, yet some members may also display less enthusiasm and more impatience with your leadership or with themselves. Attendance may suffer. Sometimes this transition period may be marked by a struggle for control of the group. This struggle may be subtle and smoldering and may erupt later into full conflict. During this stage, members will increasingly face such questions as, *How much will I disclose about myself? Is this really a safe place? Will people reject me? What do they think of me so far?* They may also enter into conflicts with one another, label people as "problem cases," or refuse to trust the group. Naturally, the group leader needs to be prepared for a challenge of his leadership.

The best way to handle this conflict is to deal with it openly and honestly. If you ignore, discount, or fight the challenge, you are actually modeling behaviors which contradict the intention of the group—the development of trust which leads to change. For example, you might begin by saying, "I detect some conflict here, what do you all think?" As you discuss the issue, your honesty, lack of defensiveness, and acceptance of people will provide a constructive model for the group. In general, you can help members move through this stage by dealing sensitively with negative feelings. This involves resolving conflicts as well as encouraging people as they make progress.

STAGE THREE: WORKING

Group members in this stage are thinking, *Let's accomplish something together.* They are willing to work as they grow together. Cohesiveness is the distinguishing mark of this stage. Other traits of this stage include the following:

Trust and acceptance. Members trust one another and the leader. Trust is evident by their willingness to take risks in talking about their personal concerns.

Empathy and caring. Members display their care by a deep and subjective understanding of one another's situations.

Hope. Members desire change and believe that it is attainable.

Commitment to change. Members grow when they know what to change and how to go about it. Commitment is evident when individuals follow through with their plans to make things different.

Intimacy. People feel liked and they like one another; they feel close to one another.

Self-disclosure. Members are honest with one another about what they think, feel, and do.

Conflict resolution. The inevitable disagreements and hurt feelings are discussed or resolved appropriately.

For all the positive elements of the working stage, at least three pitfalls exist. First, your group may become a closed group at this point. Everyone may have agreed from the outset to keep the group open to new people, but the group can effectively close itself to outsiders in practice when members develop the attitude, *No one knows and understands me like the people in this group, and other people will only get in the way of deepening our relationships.* If this occurs, bring it to the attention of the group. For example, you could say, "It's my impression that we've drifted from our concern to include new people in the group. What do you all think?" "What in our attitudes encourages a closed stance?" "How can we rekindle our desire to minister to new people?"

Secondly, your group may become comfortable with each other to such a degree that individual growth stops. Members quit challenging one another as they lose their intensity to change. As a result, the group can lose its focus and purpose for existence. Your role as a leader is to continue to provide a balance between encouragement and challenge, between comfort and confrontation.

Evaluation Questions

1. Review the elements of an effective group environment listed below. Put a check mark beside the two elements you feel will be the easiest for you to establish.

✓ ✗
❑ ❑ Love and acceptance________________

❑ ❑ Safety and trust________________

❑ ❑ Empathy and comfort________________

❑ ❑ Hope and encouragement________________

❑ ❑ Power and control________________

❑ ❑ Openness and honesty________________

❑ ❑ Freedom of expression ________________

❑ ❑ Information and perspective________________

Now, place an "✗" beside the ones you feel will be the hardest for you to establish. Lastly, for those elements you marked with an "X," write down a couple of ways you can improve your ability to establish that element.

2. Rate yourself on the following group leader traits and skills.

	low				high
genuineness	1	2	3	4	5
nonpossessive love	1	2	3	4	5
empathy	1	2	3	4	5
active listening	1	2	3	4	5
encouraging openness	1	2	3	4	5
facilitating	1	2	3	4	5
knowing limits	1	2	3	4	5

3. Which of the three stages of a group leader's development apply to you?

   ❑ Stage One: Focus on Self

   ❑ Stage Two: Focus on Content

   ❑ Stage Three: Focus on People

   How long have you been in that stage? Have you ever gone through all the stages?

   What can you do to move to the third stage?

4. Think back upon the last group of which you were a member. At which stage did the group function most of the time?

   ❑ Stage One: exploration

   ❑ Stage Two: transition

   ❑ Stage Three: working

   What do you think kept the group at that stage?

   What could have been done to encourage the group to move to the third stage?

Motives for Group Involvement

OBJECTIVES

- to understand the reasons people join or lead groups,
- to examine the role of emotions, and
- to determine how to help your group "bond" more effectively.

People become involved in small groups, either as a member or as a leader, for a variety of conscious and unconscious reasons. Members also bring with them a variety of fears and concerns about the group itself. By under-standing how these motivations and de-motivations influence people's actions, you can better meet their needs.

Reasons People Join a Group

The following list of motivations suggests some of the conscious and unconscious needs people bring to the group.

The need to belong. Life in the metropolitan centers of our country and the rapidity with which people change jobs and residences cause a lack of depth in relational roots.

Loneliness and feelings of estrangement can creep into people's lives, so people usually join a group in order to belong. In spite of their fears, they want to be known, loved, and appreciated for who they are. Even people who have healthy family relationships desire to belong to a group of peers outside the family. They want to be part of a community.

Oftentimes, however, people are afraid to let people into their lives so they can be known and loved. They may have been hurt or seen others hurt. They are afraid of similar injury and, thus, protect themselves by holding people at a distance until they can develop trust. They will still join a group seeking love and acceptance on an unconscious level. Since we have been created with a need to be loved, people overcome loneliness by becoming involved in various groups and activities. While few will outright say, "I'm lonely; please be my friend," many will carry an unconscious motivation of wanting to belong and be loved into their group membership. They want to be known, to be loved, and to be included for who they really are.

The need to contribute. People also need to give love. As much as we are helped by knowing that others will be there for us, there is also great benefit in being able to help and support someone else. The benefit arises from the fact that as we help others, we are fulfilling our created design, and that is satisfying (Galatians 6:2). Some people have become so dependent upon others' perceptions of their contributions that they are compelled to rescue and save almost everyone who crosses their paths, but this aberration of our call to "share one another's burdens" does not nullify our need to be needed.

The need to understand. Many people who join a group need input, advice and help. They need a new perspective on life, its problems, promises, and rewards, to lead their lives more effectively. Yet many people are unaware of their need for new understanding. They may not join the group out of a conscious desire to gain insight into God and their own lives. Perhaps they may feel a general disquiet and discontentment with life; perhaps not. Many people, however, are encumbered with oppressive expectations of what they should do and who they should be, which actually retards their spiritual and personal growth.

For example, a young mother of two preschool children may feel undesirable because of the effects of bearing and raising children upon her figure and grooming. She feels insecure in her husband's love even though he remains devoted to her. She may not join a group consciously seeking insight into her feelings of unworthiness. Nonetheless, she needs to understand God's acceptance of her, the proper basis of her image of herself. In addition, she needs insight into how she has built her self-worth upon the faulty foundation of her physical appearance. In short, whether or not people consciously recognize it, they need to understand the truth as revealed in God's Word as well as the implications of that truth in their day-to-day lives.

Need to be understood. Not only do people need to understand, they need to be heard and understood. When they feel understood, they feel validated as a person of worth. For example, one young mother joined a grief support group after she had lost a child at birth. As she shared her experience of deep disappointment, confusion, and anger, the other members of the group responded with words like, "I know what you mean," "The same thing happened to me," and "I would feel the same if I were in your shoes." She felt understood and said, "I'm so glad to hear you all say these things. Before I came to this group, I felt like I was going crazy." She felt confirmed as a person with normal human responses at a time when she felt she was going out of her mind.

The need to regain control. If you are leading a group which offers the promise of recovery from some form of setback (for example, divorce, death of a family member, codependency, sexual abuse, or chemical dependency), people will join out of a desire for help. They need the support of others to recover a normal life, and they are consciously looking for that support. By providing the elements of an effective group environment, you will be giving them the ability to regain control over their lives and start putting things back together.

Reasons Why People Lead a Group

Many of the reasons that lead people to join a group also serve as motives for leading a group. Leaders also need to belong, contribute, understand, and regain control. Leading a group can fill these needs. We can help others as our own needs are being met, but less positive motivations may also contribute to our desire for group leadership, such as our desire "to be somebody" and a sense of guilt if we don't serve as a leader.

The search for significance. Some people lead groups out of a desire to feel important. For example, several college students began leading their own small group studies on eschatology, the doctrine of the last days, the "hot topic of the day." They later realized that they had unconsciously desired to be regarded as the "fount of knowledge" on a particular subject. They gained a sense of significance in being sought after for their ability to quote Scripture and answer people's questions about an interesting topic. Others may wish to climb the ladder of church leadership, build a following of their own, or be viewed as a rescuer for people in trouble. These motivations reveal a basic need for significance which is being met through group leadership.

Guilt. Unfortunately, some Christian leaders motivate their followers through guilt. People are made to feel guilty for their failures and lack of virtue. They tend to measure people's spirituality via their degree of involvement in the ministry's programs. As a result, followers who desire to grow spiritually feel they must immerse themselves in ministry activities in order to absolve their guilt. If the leader highlights the small group ministry, these individuals will gravitate toward small group leadership.

Most people express their desire to lead a group in terms of helping others, however, some of our unconscious motives may be less self-giving. Rarely can we claim completely pure motives in seeking to lead a group, but we should all be aware of reasons which may lie in the back of our minds. In this way, we can minimize our using others to accomplish self-centered goals.

Fears People Bring to a Group

Members and leaders have motives for joining a group, but they also have reasons to *avoid* the group. These mixed motives create a tension for many people. Most of our fears are unvoiced and many are even unconscious, yet their presence guides and shapes our responses to people and situations. Simply describing a fear often helps to neutralize its effects in our lives. For example, many of our relationships are guided by a fear of rejection. We may not be constantly and consciously aware of that fear, yet it prevents us from stepping out and meeting new people. Once we gain an awareness of our fear of rejection, we can then examine it and begin to control our fear instead of allowing our fear to control us. Other fears include:

Fear of being known. Even though people may be lonely, they are fearful of being known. Many people share the secret fear, *If they only knew what I was really like, they* *would not want to be my friend.* As a consequence, they reveal very little of their true thoughts and feelings. Others fear appearing foolish or ignorant, so they reluctantly speak up or invite conversations with others. You can help people overcome their fear of being known by affirming their contributions. This involves listening respectfully and appreciating their input. In addition, you can relieve pressure on them to participate in the group. This will allow them the freedom to contribute to the group when they feel comfortable.

Fear of being betrayed. People resent the betrayal of trust that occurs when something said in confidence is passed on to others. When the broken confidence is compounded by a misrepresentation of their lives to others, hurt and anger are inevitable. The pain of these experiences causes people to fear being betrayed, so they typically reveal only the aspects of their lives which are already generally known. Fear of betrayal can be eased by insisting, "The things said in the group should remain in the group," or "Let people tell their own story." This should be done in word (for example, during the reading of the ground rules) and in deed (for example, asking someone to stop telling another's story).

Fear of disappointment. We have all experienced unfulfilled hopes and dreams. As a result, we insulate ourselves from too much hope. We think, *If I expect bad things to happen, I won't be disappointed when they do.* The greater the pain people experience from dashed hopes, the greater fear they have of disappointment. As you encourage an atmosphere of hope in your group, be mindful that some members of your group may have experienced grave disappointments in their situations and relationships. Let people know that the group cannot meet their critical needs. It can only play a part in the process. Know when to refer to a professional when people's needs exceed the ability of the group. Hope for change can be kept alive when adequate resources are brought into a person's life.

Fear of change. Even when life's circumstances appear unbearable, we often fear a change in those circumstances. This is because we are familiar, at least, with the difficulties we face. Familiarity brings a measure of stability and security, painful as things may be. In addition, change often brings additional pain and is sometimes frightening. We do not know what roles we should play, what to expect from others, or what ways to find comfort.

People overcome their fear of change when they observe others risking change and making it through safely. Encourage people to talk about their experiences of growth and change, including the fears and difficulties they faced along the way. These life experiences communicate, *You can do it. It may be difficult; but with the Lord's help, you can do it.*

Fear of failure. No one wants to be a failure and to experience the resulting rejection by others. We want to be "somebody," and those who fail are "nobodies." At least this is what our culture teaches through the educational system and business world. Encourage your group members that while we may experience failure, we are not failures as a result. In other words, who we are is not dependent upon what we do. When people place their trust in Christ alone for the forgiveness of their sins, they become children of God. That is their identity. Yet, Christians still sin and God still loves and accepts them (Psalms 51, 103; Romans 5:1–2; Hebrews 4:14–16; 10:17–22). Model this love and acceptance in your group, and you will help people overcome their fear of failure.

Understanding the Role of Emotions

The issue of emotions and feelings will likely surface during the course of your group, if your members apply the truth of Scripture into the deep corners of their lives with openness and honesty. Most evangelical Christians, however, feel uncomfortable with discussions about and displays of emotions. This reservation may be rooted in a proper concern that people place their faith in the Lord and in His moral guidance, or the concern about "emotionalism" may surface out of a fear of dealing with their own painful emotions.

Through the entertainment industry and the educational system, our secular culture preaches, "If it feels good, do it," and conversely, "If it doesn't feel good, don't do it." Christians rightly should resist this teaching as a basis for godly living. In addition, God and His Word, not our emotional reactions to people and situations, are the only proper objects of our faith. Many Christians, however, have overreacted to our culture by disallowing emotions in the spiritual life. One leader observed, "In Christ I am a dead man; and dead men do not have emotions." Many who follow this dictum deny their hurt and anger and, consequently, become emotionally numb to both pain and joy.

EMOTIONS ARE OKAY

Emotions occupy a legitimate role in the Christian life. King David observes, "Surely you desire truth in the inner parts; you teach me wisdom in the inmost place" (Psalm 51:6). God wants us to be honest with what we experience deep inside us. This includes our thoughts, motives, and feelings. He desires that we deal honestly and truthfully with our emotions. In addition, we find the psalmist expressing his emotions to God as he struggles with life's circumstances. For example, David, "a man after God's own heart" (Acts 13:22), expressed his emotions to God by repeating four times the phrase, "How long?" as he waited for God's answer to his prayer (Psalm 13). He was hurting emotionally and expressed it to God. Yet, he continued to trust in God's goodness, "I will sing to the Lord, for he has been good to me." Faith and the expression of negative emotions can go together.

DEALING WITH EMOTIONS

You can properly handle your emotions as a Christian by implementing the following suggestions.

1. Identify how you truly feel about the situation you face. You may feel awkward and uncomfortable in a particular situation. You will benefit greatly if you can identify your specific feelings. For example, your general discomfort may be specifically fear or anger. Allow yourself to experience the emotion. In doing so, you take responsibility for the fact that you are indeed fearful.

   One way you can identify your emotions is through the kind of reflective prayer we read in the psalms. The psalmists descriptively recount not only their situations but their emotional reactions to those situations. Their poetry serves as a model for us as we deal with painful emotions.

2. Identify the thoughts that generate your feelings. Feelings do not occur in a vacuum. They emerge from our belief systems through which we interpret our life experiences. This is why two people can experience differing emotions as they encounter the same situation. For example, you may believe that those who fail should be rejected. Consequently, you experience fear of rejection when you show up late for work even though your supervisor is a kind and understanding person.

3. Gain God's perspective about your situation. Determine His view of who you are and what you are experiencing. Then trust Him by believing His Word instead of the elements of your belief system. For example, trust God

when He says you are completely accepted by Him (Colossians 1:21–22) even though you show up late for work.

4. Finally, trust God to change your emotions. Often our emotions change over a period of time, not instantly. Allow yourself time to adjust and lean upon God's resources as you wait on Him to change you.

Scaling the "Ladder of Intimacy"

As you prepare for your group, you should be aware that people rarely communicate on the same level of intimacy with everyone they know. In fact, one might say we scale a ladder of openness and honesty in our relationships.

The first level or step is that of casual conversation, chitchat. Examples are "Hi, how are you?" "Boy, it sure is raining today" and "This line is slow, isn't it?" The depth of intimacy approaches conversations found in elevator talk.

On the second step, we exchange facts regarding what we know. Men's conversations around the office water cooler often reflect this level. "The Cards are doing poorly in the pennant race," "The price of stocks is down," "The 1950 Chevy sure is a classic car," are examples of the fact exchange level.

An exchange of ideas occurs on the third step. On this step, we feel secure enough to tell what we think. Either we have done our homework and are able to defend our ideas, or we know the person we are talking to is not going to discount our input. Many solid friendships between American men are built on this level.

On the fourth step, we share how we feel on a wide range of issues. It goes beyond the she-makes-me-so-mad often heard in the work place to sharing an I-feel-depressed-today type of disclosure. Women often build friendships on this level; men less often.

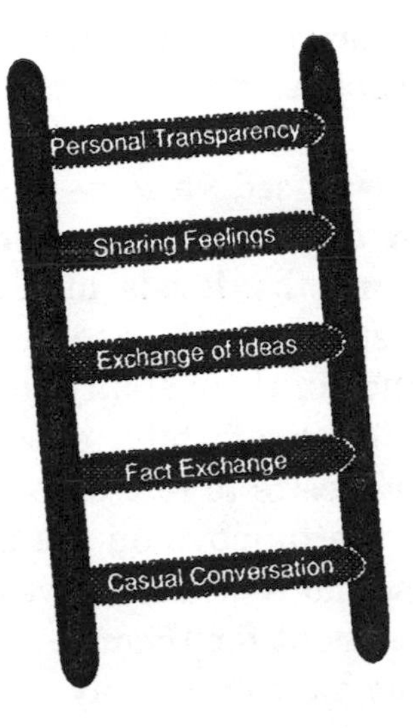

On the top step of the ladder is the exchange of dreams, hopes, fears, and failures. Personal transparency leads to a sense of being known for who you really are. True intimacy lies at this level. Sadly, most families lack this level of communication.

The climb up the ladder requires a trust that overcomes the fear of exposure and time in which to build that trust. Additionally, the higher you climb, the fewer people there are with whom you are able to share that level. We all share the level of "fact exchange" with scores of people. Yet, the time required to develop higher levels of intimacy limits the number of people with whom you can share your emotions and hopes.

People use this ladder in their interaction with groups in three ways. First, people rarely begin their group interaction on the fourth step. People often need time to warm up to a disclosure of emotions. Early in the life of your group, people will interact mostly on the lower levels of intimacy, exchanging facts and ideas along with a few emotions. As the weeks progress and trust grows, people will interact more on the higher steps. In addition, people will begin each week on the lower steps and move up the ladder as the meeting proceeds. The more mature the group, the more quickly people move to the higher levels of interaction.

Second, people also need variety—maintaining a high level of intimacy in a group is emotionally taxing and uncomfortable, so vary the levels of sharing by asking different kinds of questions.

Third, people differ in their ability to climb the ladder. Men typically do not feel comfortable above the level of idea exchange. Others may desire to remain on the level of facts. Gently encourage people to move up the ladder, but do not force them to disclose more of themselves than they wish. Provide a safe environment for them in case they decide to climb higher than they have previously attempted.

Evaluation Questions

1. Of the reasons why people join or lead a group, which ones do you think apply to you? How do these motivations affect your ability to lead an effective group?

    - ❑ The need to belong

    - ❑ The need to contribute

    - ❑ The need to understand

    - ❑ The need to be understood

    - ❑ The need to regain control

    - ❑ The need for significance

    - ❑ The need to resolve guilt

2. How would you describe your understanding of emotions in the Christian life? What are some appropriate and inappropriate ways to deal with our emotions?

3. How will you help people in your group experience and express their feelings in healthy ways?

4. List the people with whom you share the higher levels of intimacy.
   - Third Level - Exchange of Ideas
   - Fourth Level - Sharing of Feelings
   - Fifth Level - Sharing of Dreams, Hopes, and Fears

- What do you feel allows you to share these levels with these people?

- What prevents you from sharing greater intimacy with others?

5. List the names of your group members. What qualities about your group will help meet their needs?

Your Group as a Family

OBJECTIVES

- to understand how members of your group grew up in their families and how their backgrounds influence their group involvement,
- to know when the nurturing atmosphere of the group is not enough for some people and when to refer them to a professional care-giver, and
- to gain a perspective of how your group can function as the "family of God."

ONE YOUNG WOMAN RECENTLY JOINED a church after her graduation from college. When she joined a group, she said to the other members, "My parents neglected me while I was growing up. I have no brothers or sisters. You are the only people that matter to me. You are my family."

What this young woman said of her church relationships is true for all believers. The Apostle Paul explains that every Christian becomes a child of God and, therefore, brothers and sisters of Christ (Romans 8:16–17, 21, 29). He also refers to the Christian community as the "the family of believers" (Galations 6:10). Peter, likewise, addresses his readers as the "the family of God" (1 Peter 4:17). At the new birth

(John 1:12–13) every Christian becomes a member of God's family and shares a family relationship with other Christians.

This young woman's experience brings this biblical emphasis into sharper focus. Her family did not nurture her as she grew up. They fed, clothed, and housed her, took her to the doctor when she was sick, gave her presents at Christmas, and sent her to school, but they did not care for her mentally, emotionally, and spiritually. So when she started life on her own, she looked to the family of God as her source of nourishment and care. She rightly believed that the family of God is a source of redemption for those who suffer from deprivation in their human families.

Dysfunctional Families

Like this woman, many people grow up in families which do not function in healthy ways. Their families do not allow a full range of normal human behaviors, emotions, and interactions for the adults or the children. In this sense, these families are dysfunctional; they do not function as they should. Researchers have noticed certain patterns of behavior in the dysfunctional families they study. Greater levels of family dysfunction occur when these patterns are dominant. Chief among these patterns is the communication of a predictable set of messages.

DO NOT FEEL

Dysfunctional families do not allow children to feel. Either through a lack of modeling of proper emotional behavior or through punishment for any display of emotions, dysfunctional families do not allow their children to feel their emotions. For example, a child who grows up in a home where his parents do not express any emotion, negative or positive, will have great difficulty in dealing with his own emotions. Additionally, if a child is consistently punished when he displays anger, for example, he will learn to repress any angry feelings he encounters as an adult. Many adults experience great difficulty with their emotions because during childhood they heard such refrains as, "Big girls don't cry," "Don't be a sissy, son; quit crying," or "You shouldn't feel that way."

DO NOT TRUST

Children from dysfunctional families do not learn to trust. Children cannot learn trust in an unstable environment. The instability may be caused by the father's chronic job changing, by a serious illness of a parent, or by a parent's drinking behavior. Divorce, emotional and legal, also creates instability for a child. In addition, some parents simply neglect their children by not caring about how they get home from school, whether they stay out late at night, or what kind of friends they have. Simple gestures can teach a child to trust or not to trust. For example, if a father forgets a promised trip to the playground and makes no effort to make it up, his children learn to distrust their father's word.

DO NOT TALK

Those who grow up in dysfunctional families learn to not talk. Any group of people living together must talk, but they may talk on a superficial level only. In dysfunctional families, children are not allowed to express in words what they think or feel. They certainly are not allowed to talk about the real problems the family may face. For example, if a family is evicted from their apartment because the father has gambled away the rent check, the children are not likely to be allowed to point out the problem (i.e., Dad). They may be allowed to talk about the weather as they watch their belongings soak up the rain on the sidewalk. But family rules do not allow anyone to criticize Dad. If someone does criticize him, he is quickly and severely condemned.

Many parents teach their children not to talk by such

comments as, "Children should be seen and not heard," "I didn't ask you what you think; just do what I said," or "Don't talk back to your father."

DO NOT TOUCH

Finally, dysfunctional families do not allow children to touch appropriately. Some children are touched only when they are being spanked or physically abused. Others are simply never cuddled by their parents. Still others never see their parents hug or kiss. These children do not learn to touch appropriately. Many American men are taught while growing up that men do not touch (unless while shaking hands, playing contact sports, or seeking sex). Thus, they have trouble expressing affection both to women and other men. Many girls are sexually abused, either through the acts of a stranger or, more likely, through incest. They also have great difficulty expressing affection; they are unsure of what constitutes proper touching.*

Note: You may want more understanding about the complex and confusing dynamics of dysfunctional families. We recommend *Codependency: A Christian Perspective*, *Rapha's 12-Step Program for Overcoming Codependency*, and *Getting Unstuck*.

When the Group Is Not Enough

Many of us can identify the immediate reason we hurt emotionally: someone has ignored us, rejected us, or laughed at us; we feel ashamed because we've failed or we don't look attractive; we have made mistake after mistake and our lives are wrecks. Our pain, however, is often compounded and complicated by several factors, including;

- present offenses;
- past offenses (the deep wounds of neglect, abuse, and manipulation in dysfunctional families);

* *It Will Never Happen To Me!*, Claudia Black (Denver: M.A.C., 1982).

- established dysfunctional behavior patterns (using a variety of defense mechanisms to try to feed our craving for love and respect, yet avoid the pain of failure and rejection); and
- complicating consequences (caused by poor decisions: debt, strained or broken relationships, bitterness, etc.).

The pain we feel may be blunted by the numbness some of us use to block the pain, but for many of us, our present hurts are magnified by unresolved past wounds. An analogy of this is a broken arm. When a healthy arm is thumped, there may be slight pain but it quickly subsides. When a broken arm is thumped, however, the great amount of pain is way out of proportion to the little things. Many of us are like people with broken arms: little things hurt a lot—and big blows are excruciatingly painful.

HOW THEY ACT

Common Personality Types

Understanding our personality type (our goals, desires, defenses, and ways of relating to others) can significantly help in the healing process. As we learn to identify patterns in our behavior, we can predict how we usually act in given situations. Then when we have identified our usual behavior, we can more readily *choose* how we will act. Personality theories are many and sometimes complex. For instance, most of us respond in certain ways to some types of situations, but quite differently in others depending on factors such as the nature of the relationship or the perceived level of threat or gain. Some common personality types are listed below.

- *Passive aggressive* - marked by hidden resistance to authority.
- *Dependent* - always looking to another to give direction and assume responsibility.
- *Compulsive* - excessive neatness, orderliness, and promptness; usually rigid and stingy.

- *Histrionic* - attention seeking and dramatic; usually overreact emotionally.
- *Narcissistic* - excessive self-centeredness which borders on self-love.
- *Avoidant* - aloofness and absence of personal relationships; probably excessive daydreaming.
- *Borderline* - unstable, constantly fluctuating mood. Might be said to have a "stormy" personality.
- *Paranoid* - continually suspicious and jealous. They see the worst in everything.

COMMON BEHAVIOR CHARACTERISTICS . . .

In conjunction with personality types, it is very helpful for people to identify certain behaviors. This identification serves to give perception that these behaviors may be the product of past wounds or poor choices. Also, in the context of a group, the identification and disclosure of these behaviors lets others know they are not alone. This realization often leads to help for change and real progress. Several categories of painful or destructive behavior include anxiety, depressed moods, clinical depression, and extreme behaviors.

. . . WHICH EXPRESS ANXIETY.

aggressiveness
defensiveness
excessive talking
unprovoked anger
argumentative speech
constant busyness
rapid speech
restlessness
confused speech
constant sighing
excessive bragging
exaggerating
self-centeredness
hysteria
inappropriate laughter

. . . WHICH EXPRESS A DEPRESSED MOOD.

passiveness
quietness
uncertainty
lack of facial expression
lack of activity
fearfulness
lack of confidence
lack of motivation

. . . OF CLINICAL DEPRESSION.

loss of appetite
excessive sleeping
inability to sleep
fear of death
frequent crying
confusion
listlessness
loss of facial expression
long periods of motionlessness
morbid thoughts
expressed hopelessness
excessive worry
strong guilt feelings
physical complaints
delusional thinking
thoughts of suicide

. . . OF EXTREME BEHAVIORS: DISORIENTED, ANTISOCIAL, SELF-DESTRUCTIVE.

fighting
drug or alcohol abuse
violent outbursts
isolation
sexual aggression
obsessiveness
irrational fear
hearing voices

hysteria or panic
euphoria
lawlessness
expression of open hostility
erratic thought patterns

WHEN TO REFER

As people feel more comfortable and safe in their groups, they often come to grips with hurt and anger which have been buried for years. Sometimes, the nurturing environment of the group is not enough because the person is overwhelmed by these emotions. It is important to realize when a person needs more help than his group can provide. Then, referral to a professional counselor is appropriate.

In many cases, the person can benefit from a Christian counselor. Talk to your pastor to get the names of counselors who are both thoroughly Christian and clinically astute. In some cases, however, someone in the group may need hospital care. Treatment programs for psychiatric problems or substance abuse vary greatly from facility to facility. It is very difficult to compare programs without first gaining specific information. General impressions of a treatment center through advertising, general reputation, or casual word of mouth should not be the primary reason for choosing a treatment center.

If you have any questions, we invite you to call one of our information counselors at Rapha. The toll free number is:

1 (800) 383 - HOPE

Your Group as a "Family of God"

Dysfunctional families produce adults whose inability to feel, talk, trust, and touch appropriately will affect the dynamics of your group interaction. Yet, you can help these people by allowing your group to function as the family of God.

ALLOW PEOPLE TO FEEL

Effective small groups focus not only upon ideas but on how people feel about those ideas. Someone may say, "I really don't believe that God loves me at all!" When people begin to express emotions in your group, beware of others who may feel uncomfortable with emotions. They may attempt to solve the person's problem and thereby remove the reason for his feelings. Or they may overtly say, "You shouldn't feel that way."

For example, Thomas, a young father of three, talked to a friend about his emotional struggles. As his friend allowed him to talk about how his difficulties affected him, Thomas began to cry. Another friend standing nearby felt uncomfortable and jumped into the conversation, offering advice and perspective. Almost immediately, Thomas distanced himself from his feelings and the conversation soon ended.

The advice offered by the mutual friend was biblical and the perspective helpful. But it was offered too soon. Thomas was robbed of the chance to use his feelings as a gauge of his personal belief system or to process his grief. In light of the quick advice, he reasoned that he had no just cause to feel discouraged and depressed. He was not allowed to feel. He lost the chance to use his feelings as a window into what he really believed about God and His provision.

HELP PEOPLE TO LEARN TO TRUST

By displaying the love and acceptance of God to your group members, you will provide the safety they need to learn to trust. Be consistent and maintain confidentiality. Do what you said you would do (e.g. start and end on time, cover a certain topic, return to a person's question, etc.) and let people tell their own stories. An environment with these elements of safety builds trust.

Michelle grew up in a legalistic Christian home. As an adult, she continued to worship in a rules-oriented church, yet she rarely felt accepted or loved in this community. She could not trust anyone out of a fear of failing to meet up to the strict expectations of her friends at church. After a few years, Michelle began to attend a church where people did not condemn others for their failures and she began to experience the forgiveness of God. She became a more open person as she struggled to develop relationships based upon trust.

ENCOURAGE PEOPLE TO TALK

Good questions do more than provide for a good group discussion. They allow people the chance to express their ideas and thoughts. When you listen, you communicate that what others say is important to you. More importantly, you affirm that people are important. Keep in mind that conversation and discussion have differing degrees of value. Many people from dysfunctional families are comfortable with an exchange of facts, but dysfunctional families create a fear of talking about ideas, opinions, and dreams. By encouraging good discussion in your group, you can help people move up that ladder of intimacy and talk about real issues and answers.

One specific way you can help people from dysfunctional families is to deal with conflict in the group. Most group leaders dread the day conflict surfaces in their groups, but if you handle the conflict properly, you can model good communication. As people learn that they can express their ideas, disagree with other people's ideas, and still walk away friends, they will be better able to manage conflict in their marriages and work relationships.

ALLOW APPROPRIATE TOUCH AMONG YOUR GROUP MEMBERS

Social norms define appropriate touch. Your modeling of proper touch can encourage appropriate displays of affection and compassion. Exercise caution when encouraging touch. Do not force people to touch others. Beware of your own need for touch and using your group to meet that need.

For example, having group members hug the person next to them out of your need to hug and be hugged is inappropriate.

In short, you can create an environment in which people from dysfunctional families can learn to enter into healthy relationships. You can help others heal the hurts in their own lives (and we all have hurts). You can also help them raise their own children or grandchildren in a healthy, biblical way.

Evaluation Questions

The members of your group will bring emotional, spiritual, and relational "baggage" from their backgrounds into the group meetings. Their sense of compulsion, denial, guilt, shame, anger, hopelessness, loneliness, and other characteristics are often traced to relationships in their families, as well as other past and present relationships.

It is no surprise that you bring some baggage, too. Sometimes a group member may treat you the way a hurtful parent or sibling treated you. Instead of responding to the situation with objectivity and healthy detachment, you may find it easy to react to that group member in the same way that you have reacted to your parent or sibling.

We want you to be aware of the dynamics of past relationships in your life so that you can anticipate how you can respond positively to the people in your group. These questions are designed to help you analyze your family and its effects, both positive and negative, on you.

FAMILY ANALYSIS

1. What were the strengths and weaknesses of your family when you were growing up?

2. Were any of these characteristics present in your family?

Addictions:
- ❑ problem drinking
- ❑ alcoholism
- ❑ drug addiction
- ❑ workaholism
- ❑ eating disorders
- ❑ gambling addiction
- ❑ sexual addiction
- ❑ success or money addiction
- ❑ other addiction

Other dysfunctional characteristics:
- ❑ divorce
- ❑ neglect
- ❑ "smothering by parent"
- ❑ verbal abuse
- ❑ emotional abuse
- ❑ physical abuse
- ❑ sexual abuse
- ❑ psychosomatic illness
- ❑ domineering father/passive mother
- ❑ loss of memory
- ❑ domineering mother/passive father
- ❑ depression
- ❑ constant tension/anxiety
- ❑ other________________

3. Describe your relationship with your father (pros and cons).

4. Describe your relationship with your mother (pros and cons).

5. Describe your relationship with each of your siblings (pros and cons).

6. Describe how these relationships affected you regarding:

a healthy self-esteem	anger
experiencing forgiveness	guilt
expressing forgiveness	critical of others
love	hate
accurate perceptions	black and white perspective of people or situations
the ability to set limits	being overly responsible
being responsible for your behavior	irresponsibility
good bonding in relationships	loneliness
free to express your feelings, ideas, decisions	being a puppet/people pleaser
ability to have fun	stiff or depressed
ability to talk, feel, and trust	repressed emotions explosions of anger

7. What **strengths** have been built into your life as a result of your family background?

8. What **weaknesses** or needs have developed in your life as a result of your family background?

9. How will these strengths and weaknesses affect your leadership/relationships with people in the group? (How will you respond when people dominate, withdraw, disagree, fawn over you, etc.?)

10. What have you learned about yourself and your family from this analysis?

11. How can you be better prepared to lead your group in light of this analysis?

12. How will you know when you need to refer someone to a professional? (What "warning signs" will you look for?)

Uniquenesses of Support Groups

OBJECTIVES

- to provide insight about nuances of support groups,
- to understand the particular style of the 12-Step approach, and
- to provide clear direction for beginning a 12-Step group.

GROWTH GROUPS ARE DESIGNED to cover topics which are common to virtually all of us. They are usually limited in their duration, and they are usually open to anyone who wants to attend at any time. Support groups, however, are significantly different in their topic, time frame, purpose, and style.

Topics

Subject matter for support groups focuses on a particular difficulty, disorder, addiction, or relational dysfunction in people's lives. Those who experience these traumas need each other's understanding and encouragement. Some of these problems center on particular addictive disorders. Twelve-Step programs have been specifically designed to help people with these problems, including:

chemical dependency;
codependency;
anorexia;
bulimia; and
compulsive overeating
sexual addiction

Other problems are not primarily addictive, but are nonetheless devastating. Support groups on these issues usually do not use the 12-Step approach:

- sexual abuse (including incest and rape victims)
- grief
- divorce recovery
- infertility
- depression
- parents of rebellious teenagers
- war veterans (post-traumatic stress disorder victims)
- unemployment

Characteristics of Support Groups

TIME FRAME

The depth of the wounds and the severity of the compulsiveness of most of these problems lends to a longer group duration than growth groups. Some groups may meet for 4–6 months, but others may choose to meet for 1–2 years.

Though many 12-Step groups are ongoing, recent studies show that most people benefit from having some time limit on the the group. The limit gives them additional motivation to take steps of progress in their choices and relationships. If they need additional time in a group, they may then choose to join the group for the next cycle.

ENVIRONMENT OF TRUST

Many therapists and support group facilitators agree that the environment created in the group is as important as the content. Most people who join a support group are deeply wounded; their trust has been seriously violated. The process of recovery, in fact, is directly linked to the growth in a person's ability to learn to trust wisely.

Facilitators can build a trusting environment by being trustworthy, stressing and modeling confidentiality, not judging people, but also, being honest and "speaking the truth in love."

PERMISSION TO FEEL

The environment of trust grants people permission to feel the hurt, anger, shame, fear, joy, and love they have repressed. Many people and families are uncomfortable and threatened by tears, but support groups are designed to provide a "safe place" so that people can get in touch with their pain.

PERSONAL RESPONSIBILITY

Each person in the group is responsible for his or her own growth. Each person moves at his own pace, not rushed or pushed by the facilitator. The environment of hope and healing then promotes the motivation and course to take steps of healing.

A corollary to personal responsibility is patience. The wounds are usually very deep. Relationships are often very complex and confused. We need to be patient with ourselves and others as we seek to follow the Lord and express His freedom and strength, and to build better behaviors and relationships.

OPEN AND CLOSED GROUPS

Confidentiality is valued in any group, but it is absolutely essential in support groups. For this reason, many facilitators chose to close their support group after an initial 3–4 week period.

If the group remains open, the facilitator must take care to let people process the fear they feel when new people join the groups. The erosion of trust is a major factor for most people in support groups. They need time to talk about these issues when their trust in the group is threatened.

Some organizations and churches have strong feelings and philosophies about the relative value of closed and open groups. The following summarizes the benefits and liabilities of each one:

OPEN GROUPS (new members may join the group at any time)

Benefits:

- accessibility to the group for those who need help
- new group members often stimulate discussion
- makes outreach one of the purposes of the group

Liabilities:

- including new people in an existing, functioning group threatens confidentiality
- limits self-disclosure until new people are trusted
- people with quite divergent needs (thought disorders, psychotic, depressed, chemical dependency, etc.) can join and thereby, dilute and confuse the group dynamics
- these factors require more group leadership skills for the group to function well

CLOSED GROUPS

Benefits:

- confidentiality is more easily kept
- trust among group members is more rapidly developed
- limiting variables (new members, diverse needs) makes the group easier to manage

Liabilities:

- the group can become ingrown; a clique can develop
- the group dynamics can become stagnant
- if people drop out for any reason, the size of the group may become too small for good dynamics

Suggestions:

a. Screen those joining the group to narrow the range of needs. The screening can be accomplished by a clear labeling of the group and a clear statement of the scope and purpose of the group.

b. Time limits for the duration of the group can aid dynamics whether the group is open or closed. Six months, nine months, or one year are recommended before a new cycle begins, though sexual abuse groups may cycle every two years.

c. Closed groups can be open for the first three to four weeks, then open for two to four weeks every six months. This allows the periodic infusion of new people without eroding the long-term dynamic of trust.

d. Open groups can use the entrance of new people to talk about trust issues. New people then serve as an opportunity for growth, not a hindrance.

DECENTRALIZATION

In growth groups, the leader takes responsibility of teaching part of the time and leading the group discussion. In a support group, each member assumes greater responsibility to contribute. That's why the leader is called "a facilitator." His role is to help each person share feelings and communicate about his or her life.

QUALIFICATIONS

One of the primary qualifications of support group facilitators is that they have experienced the difficulty which is the topic for the group, and that they have experienced significant recovery and healing. Recently, a cancer support group disbanded because the members felt misunderstood and unsupported. The facilitator had never been a cancer patient, and though she was a compassionate woman, she couldn't "connect" with the people in the group.

The severity of pain and relational problems makes it necessary that the facilitator understand the limits of his and the group's ability to meet people's needs. Occasionally, someone in the group experiences depression, a relapse into addictive behavior, abuse from a spouse, divorce, or some other problem which requires professional help. Facilitators need to understand when people need this level of help, and they can then refer people to appropriate, qualified professionals.

STYLES OF LEADERSHIP

Most support groups promote a lot of sharing by group members without probing questions or confrontation by the facilitator. People come to tell their story and to hear others. Some facilitators, however, choose a style which includes occasional probing questions to stimulate reflection. If both probing and confrontation are used, the group has become a therapy group, not a support group.

Distinctives of the 12-Step Approach

One distinctive of 12-Step groups is that they allow people the opportunity to proceed at their own pace. Members of the groups typically share what they have learned since the last meeting, so one person may tell how he has wrestled with an issue in Step 2 while another may describe her journey in Step 7. One person may proceed quickly at one point while another may need more time to reflect on those same truths. This flexibility allows each member to personalize the content and the pace of involvement.

A second distinctive of the 12-Step approach is the comprehensive nature of the material. The 12-Steps have been accurately described as a "path of repentance" taking someone . . .

- from denial to realization of problems,
- to a sense of responsibility for those problems,
- to forgiveness, restitution, and reconciliation, and
- to a new lifestyle of healthy decisions and relationships.

This comprehensive approach avoids the "hit or miss" methods that may be meaningful at a certain point but leave people "stuck" in the process of healing and development.

Most 12-Step groups provide sponsors for new members. Even in other types of support groups, it is often very helpful to have someone a "little farther down the road" to act as an encourager and mirror to give hope and insight to those making new and difficult choices.

How to Lead a 12-Step Group

CONTENT

The actual content of 12-Step group meetings can be quite varied. As already mentioned, one of the most popular methods is to have each person share what he or she is learning. Then other people can comment and reinforce that person's progress. A second method is to teach and interact on specific topics such as forgiveness, control, hurt, anger, concept of God, etc. A third option is to have members open their 12-Step workbooks to a particular Step and all go through it together. Fourth, sometimes the group may need to have a business meeting. The content of that meeting will cover functional issues such as refreshments, collections, splitting the group if it grows too large, and other related topics.

Any of these four types of content can fit into the two following formats.

FORMATS

TRADITIONAL FORMAT

1. Quiet moment (1 min.).
2. Read Opening Group Remarks & Prayer (1 min.).
3. Read Rapha's 12-Steps (3 min.).
4. Welcome new members & guests. Ask new members to introduce themselves if they wish (3–10 min.).
5. Introduce facilitator and/or speaker for the group (2 min.).
6. Pass collection and prayer basket (1 min.).
7. Announcements (1 min.).
8. Coffee break (5 min.).
9. Content for the week (45–60 min.).
10. Read "Declaration" (1 min.).
11. Close with the "Lord's Prayer." Stand and hold hands (1 min.).

Optional Format

1. Read Opening Group Remarks & Prayer (1 min.).

2. Read Rapha's 12-Steps (3 min.).

3. Welcome new members & guests (3–10 min.).

4. Introduce facilitator and/or speaker for the group (2 min.).

5. Coffee break (5 min.).

6. Pass collection and prayer basket (1 min.).

7. Announcements (1 min.).

8. Content for the week (45–60 min.).

9. Close with the prayer (1 min.).

Note: Please give a copy of this outline to all group leaders prior to starting the session. A group leader is any person you have asked to take part in the group session.

OPENING GROUP REMARKS

(To be read by the facilitator—or someone appointed by the facilitator.)

Hello: my name is ______________ and I am your leader for tonight.

This group is a fellowship of Christians who share experiences, strength, and hope with each other so that we might solve our common problems and grow in Christ.

We recover by being honest with ourselves and others. We define honesty as "freedom from self-deception" based upon a sincere desire to recover. This desire to recover binds us together so that we become willing to admit our wrongs and deal with others as we would have them deal with us.

Before we begin our sharing, I would like for you to know that we keep everything said here tonight confidential and in this room. Please attempt to use "I" messages instead of "you" messages, as we refrain from giving advice. My role as facilitator is to guide our topic, question, or your story around this circle. I may find it necessary to move the conversation on in order that all may have time to share. We plan to close at ______________, but in case we run over, feel free to leave.

Please remember that this is a non-smoking group and that you should refrain from smoking while on church grounds.

Let's pray:

Dear Lord, by coming together to share our pain, may we minister to each other as your Holy Spirit reveals truth and healing to each heart and mind. In Jesus' name we pray. Amen.

This declaration can be read during the group meeting. (See the traditional and optional formats.)

Declaration

Because of Christ's redemption,
I am a new creation of infinite worth.

I am deeply loved,
I am completely forgiven,
I am fully pleasing,
I am totally accepted by God.
I am absolutely complete in Christ.

When my performance reflects my new identity in Christ,
that reflection is dynamically unique.

There has never been another person like me
in the history of mankind,
nor will there ever be.
God has made me an original,
one-of-a-kind, a special person.

Note: The facilitator should give a copy of this declaration to each person before it is read by the group.

Evaluation Questions

1. Do you plan to lead a support group? If so, what topic will your group address?

2. Examine the characteristics of support groups? Describe your plan for each one:

   Time Frame

   Environment of trust

   Permission to feel

   Personal responsibility

   Open and closed groups

3. If you plan to lead a 12-Step group, which format will your group use? Why?

Managing Difficulties

OBJECTIVE

- to give suggestions for dealing with potential difficulties.

WHENEVER YOU GATHER a group of people together you will encounter difficulties. Some of them are minor and easily managed. Some, however, require a bit more training and input. Some of the more common problems are addressed in this chapter.

The following situations can prove a real challenge to leaders and facilitators. They are explained on the following pages.

- Someone talks too much.
- The silent person.
- No one will talk.
- A group member consistently argues.
- Conflicts.
- Someone uses offensive language.
- People talk about inappropriate topics.
- A group participant comes to the group obviously inebriated or under the influence of drugs.

- The group leader starts feeling anxious, angry, codependent, or "burned out"
- It becomes evident that confidentiality has been broken
- Group participants are romantically attracted to each other, and this comes to the attention of the group leader
- A group participant, very early in recovery, decides to start his own ministry to help other addicts
- A group participant insists that he/she doesn't need to do all of this "recovery stuff" because Jesus has brought about the cure
- People use "cross-talk"
- People give advice
- People express excessive emotionality
- Someone needs child care
- Pastor-bashing

Now let's look at each of these in more detail.

SOMEONE TALKS TOO MUCH

Sometimes you will have members of your group who will dominate the group discussion. They may talk excessively about themselves, tell very detailed stories, or even direct the group discussion in a different direction than the one you planned. In effect, they will control the tenor and agenda of the group.

Excessive talkers will drain the life of a group. First, no one has an opportunity to contribute while they are talking. Second, group members will come to resent his or her comments and behaviors. Finally, excessive talkers tend to steer the group discussion away from feelings and in-depth responses toward a more superficial level of interaction.

As the leader, you need to deal with the situation created by the excessive talker. You can begin with a subtle approach, but later you may need to be more direct. Always keep in mind that excessive talkers are trying to get attention from others.

First, look for breaks in the person's comments, either in his ideas or simply when he takes a breath. Quickly ask the group, "What do the rest of you think?" After some group response, move on to another issue or point in the discussion. If this fails to involve others in the discussion, try saying, "I know what you're saying, but let's hear what some others have to say."

Finally, you may have to speak to the person after the group meeting and say something like, "I appreciate your comments and I'm glad you feel free to participate in the discussion. However, I'd like you to limit your comments so others can contribute as well." The person may experience hurt feelings, so be as gentle as you are firm.

As your group leading skills improve and the group matures, you can help excessive talkers by raising in the group the issues they create. The goal is not to put them in their place, but to help them to understand why they talk so much and to gain insight into how their talkativeness affects others. Excessive talkers are often unaware of how their conversational style is perceived by others. Dealing with the issue in the group can help excessive talkers grow.

You may say something like, "Terry, I cannot help but notice that you contribute much more than the others to the group discussion. Why do you think that's so?" After the person's response, you can say to the group, "How do the rest of you perceive Terry's role in our discussions?"

This approach should only be done in a group where trust has been established. Where trust is undeveloped, talkative people will not be receptive to others' observations, and other group members will become very cautious in their group involvement.

THE SILENT PERSON

Compared to the excessive talker, the silent person may seem like a blessing to some leaders, yet silent people also have needs which can be met in the group. Silent people may be resistant or shy. Because of their sense of shame, they may feel like they have nothing worthwhile to say. They may fear looking foolish or being rejected. Whatever the case, they use silence as a means of withdrawing from the group.

Do not pressure them to contribute or criticize them for their silence. Instead, encourage their participation by listening to, appreciating, and affirming their comments. You may wish to approach them privately or in the group and let them know that some people may misinterpret their silence. Ask them what their silence means and how you can encourage their participation.

NO ONE WILL TALK

Sometimes the entire group seems subdued and unresponsive. There may be many reasons for this emotional lethargy or blockage. Perhaps the trust level has not developed in the group. People may fear that what is shared will be disclosed outside the meeting. Maybe everyone has just had a hard day and wants to listen. Rather than "force" the group, you may consider several options:

- Ask the group why they are quiet.
- Offer to pray for the group, and then teach a relevant concept without requiring much interaction. You may want to invite each person to read a paragraph or two from the book or workbook. Discussion is allowed, but not necessary. These groups can be restful and can lead to greater group cohesiveness.
- Consider playing a tape of a recovering person, or playing a tape which will be meaningful to the group.

While these alternatives are not to be used often, they occasionally provide relief for a tired group.

A GROUP MEMBER CONSISTENTLY ARGUES

A group member's anger may surface in the form of constant criticism, negative comments, or arguing. You may want to pursue the person by asking him what caused the underlying anger, or by allowing feedback from the group.

If this situation persists, it may be necessary to discuss the problem with the group coordinator or the pastor. Usually when someone is very argumentative, he or she is feeling threatened. While this person may need special attention, it is unwise to sacrifice the group dynamic and progress.

CONFLICTS

As people begin discussing their lives and responses in the group, you may notice them saying things like, "You shouldn't feel that way," "You frustrate me," or "You don't care!" Ironically, this can be a positive sign—members are becoming more free in their communication. At this point, you can direct this freedom by encouraging people to take responsibility for their own emotions. You can do this by encouraging members to talk in terms of "I" and not "you."

For example, "I feel angry when you say . . . to me" is preferred to "YOU make me angry when you say . . . to me." Other examples include, "I feel frustrated when you . . . ." "I don't perceive that you care" or "I feel hurt when . . . ."

This approach will not eliminate conflict, but it will contribute to your ability to manage the conflict so that it does not rupture the group. In addition, group members will learn effective and constructive skills in dealing with conflicts they face outside the group.

SOMEONE USES OFFENSIVE LANGUAGE

When some people "get in touch" with the pain in their lives, their anger, hurt, and resentment toward the offenders can trigger coarse language or cursing. Some facilitators respond to such language in extreme ways. Some may try to show their identification with the person by using profanity, too. Others, on the other extreme, may tell the swearing person "not to ever use language like that in the group again."

We recommend the following guidelines for handling profanity and coarse language:

- Don't condemn the person. Very few of us express the pain and anger of deep wounds with perfect control of voice tone and choice of words. One of the main goals of a support group is to stimulate honesty and vulnerability, and it is usually counterproductive to the group environment to tell people not to talk in certain ways.
- In most cases, simply ignore the profanity or coarse language. If the facilitator models clean and appropriate (but occasionally intense) speech, the other members of the group will probably follow that example.
- If someone consistently offends group members by profane language, you may choose to either ask the group how they feel about the offensive language (using "I" statements, of course), or talk to the person privately to express your appreciation for his or her openness and your desire that the tone of the group be conducive to participation by all members. You can explain that the person's willingness to share openly is a great asset to the group, but it would be an even greater asset if more appropriate expressions could be used.

With all of the crushed identities, twisted relationships, distorted perceptions, aberrant and self-destructive behavior, and intense, unresolved emotions in group members' lives, remember to "major on the majors," that is, focus on the things that are really important. When Jesus spent time with tax gatherers and sinners, He made them feel comfortable and uncondemned so that the Spirit could do His work in their lives.

PEOPLE TALK ABOUT INAPPROPRIATE TOPICS

Invariably someone in the group will bring up a subject which should not be discussed in a group. For example, they may reveal confidential information or describe their sexual behaviors too graphically. The group leader should be prepared to deal with the problem. For example, you can say, "I can understand your desire to talk about this. However, this might not be a good time. Others in the group might feel uncomfortable and we may be breaching confidentiality. I'd like to talk about this with you later, if you wish."

A GROUP PARTICIPANT COMES TO THE GROUP INEBRIATED OR UNDER THE INFLUENCE OF DRUGS

The level of intoxication will determine how you should handle this kind of situation. If the member is manageable, it would be wise to ask a co-facilitator or member of the core group to meet with him individually during the group time. Make sure that transportation is provided. This is an opportunity to plant seeds for intervention and intensive treatment. The group member may be ready for professional help. You should allow time for the group to process their own feelings about this incident. Typically, group participants will either be angry at the relapser or feel that they are at fault for not preventing the relapse. The fear that they, too, could relapse often underlies these feelings. End the group with prayer for the relapsed person.

THE GROUP LEADER STARTS FEELING ANXIOUS, ANGRY, CODEPENDENT, OR "BURNED OUT"

Burnout is one of the most common experiences of both professional and lay persons in the recovery field. Chemically dependent people, those with eating disorders, codependents, victims of abuse, and grief sufferers are typically very intense and needy, and it is easy to lose perspective when working with them. Signs of burnout include:

- persistent irritation and anger at relatively insignificant things;
- an overwhelming sense of need to caretake the needy people in the group;

- thinking obsessively about what has gone on in the groups;
- feeling hopeless;
- feeling personally responsible when someone has relapsed;
- feeling that you are the only one who can do this work; and
- sleep disturbance.

There are many other signs of this type of stress. It is important not to ignore them. The psyche is trying to say *Take a break!* Make certain that you stay in contact with the pastor and other support group leaders. It may be necessary for you to take a leave of absence from the group and let someone else lead for a while.

IT BECOMES EVIDENT THAT CONFIDENTIALITY HAS BEEN BROKEN

Nothing is more destructive to a support group than gossip. Sometimes it is helpful to have each group participant verbally commit to the confidentiality of the group. The desire to break confidentiality is usually an ego issue, resulting from a desire to show others that you are "in the know." This can be particularly deadly in church settings where rationalizations are used, such as: "God told me to share it," or "I felt his wife had a right to know what he has been doing." If there is a significant confidentiality breach in the group, have the group process the breach of trust, and then encourage confidentiality again. After such a breach, it will take time to develop trust again.

GROUP PARTICIPANTS ARE ROMANTICALLY ATTRACTED TO EACH OTHER

While other people's behavior cannot be controlled, it is appropriate at various times in the duration of these groups to talk about what 12-Step groups call "13th stepping." This occurs when people focus on romantic or sexual feelings toward someone else in the group, rather than on their own recovery. When someone feels stronger emotionally, many intense emotions surface which may have been deadened for a while. It is natural to want to act on these feelings. However, it is a rule of thumb to avoid making any major decisions during the first year of recovery. The first year should be spent focusing on personal recovery and beginning to help others. It has been proven over the years that intense romantic involvements early in recovery, quick marriages, and divorces all take their toll on the recovering person. Often they lead to relapse. While the facilitator cannot force the person in the group to believe this principle, it is still wise to state it often.

A GROUP PARTICIPANT VERY EARLY IN RECOVERY DECIDES TO START HIS OWN MINISTRY TO HELP OTHER ADDICTS OR CODEPENDENTS

Encourage the participant to take the log out of his own eye before he tries to help other needy people recover. It is actually a form of denial to "carry the message" too soon. Focusing on his own recovery should be primary. Even the Apostle Paul had to wait years after his Damascus Road experience before beginning his missionary work. Addicts, alcoholics, people with eating disorders, victims of sexual abuse, and codependents are no different. Confronting a victim, addict, or codependent who says he has a direct message from God can be a sensitive issue, however, the way he presents the message usually shows the attitude of his heart. He may be extremely intense or even hysterical.

A GROUP PARTICIPANT INSISTS THAT HE DOESN'T NEED TO DO ALL OF THIS "RECOVERY STUFF" BECAUSE JESUS HAS BROUGHT ABOUT THE CURE

Actually, this may be true. There are certainly cases of people being instantly freed from an addiction such as alcoholism or drug abuse without the usual withdrawal symptoms. That "healing" may be truly miraculous, but it's only part of the story. They then need to deal with the severely distorted thinking patterns, harmful behaviors, strained relationships, and painful consequences of their addiction. Whether or not the person chooses to take advantage of the group is his choice. It may take time for it to become clear whether this person has actually been delivered, or whether he is using hyper-religiosity as a form of denial, in which case relapse will probably occur. The important thing to remember here is that arguing will not work. The purpose of this group is to make the support group easily available as a tool for recovery.

PEOPLE USE "CROSS-TALK"

Cross-talk occurs when individuals speak out of turn and interrupt one another. The group is disrupted, and it loses its focus of respect for the member whose turn it is to speak. Because these groups are so full of "caretakers," sometimes they can degenerate into rapid-fire discussions where the format can be lost. This is destructive to the very necessary structure of the group and is discouraged. Sometimes it may be helpful to define, describe, and explain the harmful effects of cross-talk in the group.

PEOPLE GIVE ADVICE

The very purpose of a growth or support group is to provide people with solutions for life. This should be even more true for a biblically-based group, yet solutions suggested too quickly through the giving of advice can hamper effective problem solving in at least three ways.

First, those who experience difficulties in life need to come to terms with their losses. Major difficulties and, to a lesser extent compounding minor hassles, result from or contribute to the death of hopes and dreams. Dealing with these losses takes time. Quick advice often short-circuits this process.

Second, it is better to learn how to solve problems than to have someone give you the answer. Advice givers, in effect, attempt to solve others' problems. Their advice may be sound, but the way they give it does not help people learn how to construct solutions for themselves. The familiar maxim is quite applicable, "If I give you a fish, you will eat for a day; if I teach you to fish, you will eat for a lifetime."

Third, quick advice is often superficial. While it appears to answer the problems, in reality, it does not deal with the significant issues. Biblical answers are profound, but they can be used in a simplistic way when people lack wisdom and insight about applying these truths.

If people in your group are prone to offering advice, consider having them discuss the implications of the following proverbs.

> Like one who takes away a garment on a cold day, or like vinegar poured on soda, is one who sings songs to a heavy heart.
>
> Proverbs 25:20

> He who answers before listening—that is his folly and his shame.
>
> Proverbs 18:13

> Reckless words pierce like a sword, but the tongue of the wise brings healing.
>
> Proverbs 12:18

> A simple man believes anything, but a prudent man gives thought to his steps.
>
> Proverbs 14:15

Some implications you can suggest to the group include:

- offer advice only when you have taken time to understand, mentally and emotionally, the person's condition;
- offer advice only when you have taken time to consider the implications of your advice; and
- do not offer advice in an effort to get people to "cheer up."

Caretakers tend compulsively to advise other hurting persons. However, real recovery comes not from receiving advice, but from being willing to surrender to the Lord, to grieve the wounds of the past and present, and to utilize other tools of recovery and renewal. It may be necessary to gently, but regularly, reinforce the fact that members are encouraged to share their own experience, strength, and hope, without giving advice to others.

Though advice should not be given unless it is requested, feedback provides a sense of reality to people in the group. An important benefit of a group is the opportunity to see yourself through another person's eyes. As a group member expresses his thoughts and feelings, others in the group gain impressions about the one speaking based on both verbal and nonverbal communication. When honest feedback is offered in response, the one sharing is able to find out how other people see him. The results are sometimes quite surprising and usually helpful to everyone in the group.

Sometimes, however, people in the group volunteer this feedback in a destructive way. Instruct the group that feedback should only be given when requested. For example, Sally may be telling everyone how much she resents her ex-husband. Janet desires to contribute her own observations and should ask, "May I give you feedback on what you're saying?" Only if Sally agrees is Janet free to say something like, "I perceive that you are not willing to forgive your ex-husband for causing you so much trouble. Is that the case?"

PEOPLE EXPRESS EXCESSIVE EMOTIONALITY

Wounded people have often denied their painful feelings for so long that starting to look at their pain is the equivalent of "breaking the dam" in terms of tears and painful feelings. While crying and expressing feelings in meetings is encouraged, it is important to continue with the group. Provide a box of kleenex for the group. Let the person express emotions, and give support by thanking the person for trusting the group with his or her honesty.

The danger in these situations is less for the hurting person who is letting go of repressed pain, and more for the other people in the group who are triggered to try to "rescue" such a person. It is dangerous to do "caretaking" rather than "caregiving" in a situation like this.

SOMEONE NEEDS CHILD CARE

No children should be allowed in the meetings. It can not only be detrimental for the child to be in an intense emotional meeting, but can also impede true sharing for other members. The group may decide to use part of the group finances to pay for a sitter.

"PASTOR-BASHING"

The group may begin to criticize the church leadership because the members have felt lonely and unloved in the church. When these people begin to feel loved in your group, some may begin to express attitudes such as, "Why hasn't the church met my needs like this before? I've attended this church for over five years and this is the first time someone has shown me what love is all about." Some members may begin to "bash the pastor." "Why hasn't Rev. Jones taught us these truths before? He doesn't know anything about *real* issues in people's lives!" Recognize that this criticism of the church and pastor is off-handedly flattering to you ("You've succeeded where all others have failed."). Resist the temptation to indulge or even promote this criticism and flattery. Challenge the group to consider, "It seems we're bitter or resentful toward the church leadership. What do you think?" "What does this say about us?"

Evaluation Questions

Which of the following potential difficulties are the hardest for you to manage? Rate your answer on a scale of 0 (No problems!) to 10 (Imminent catastrophe!).

What do you need to do in order to deal with each one (e.g., increase skills, gain experience, or overcome a fear of failure, a desire to be liked, or a need to rescue people from their problems)?

_____ Someone talks too much
_____ The silent person
_____ No one will talk
_____ A group member consistently argues
_____ Conflicts
_____ Someone uses offensive language
_____ People talk about inappropriate topics
_____ A group participant comes to the group inebriated or under the influence of drugs
_____ The group leader starts feeling anxious, angry, codependent, or "burned out"
_____ It becomes evident that confidentiality has been broken
_____ Group participants are romantically attracted to each other
_____ A group participant very early in recovery decides to start his own ministry to help other addicts or codependents
_____ A group participant insists that he doesn't need to do all of this "recovery stuff" because Jesus has brought about the cure
_____ People use "cross-talk"
_____ People give advice
_____ People express excessive emotionality
_____ Someone needs child care
_____ Pastor-bashing

Questions Group Leaders Ask

OBJECTIVES

- to anticipate possible problems that may be encountered while leading a group, and
- to provide solutions for these problems.

STRANGE AND WONDERFUL THINGS CAN HAPPEN when you lead a group! When "the lights come on" in people's lives, leading or facilitating a small group is a very rewarding experience, but sometimes leading others brings confusion and discouragement. Though we cannot possibly cover all of the possible scenarios in this chapter, we will examine at least a few common problems and give some practical suggestions.

WHAT TO DO WHEN . . .

. . . YOU DON'T HAVE CONFIDENCE IN YOUR ABILITY TO LEAD A GROUP.

Very few people who lead a group for the first time feel comfortable and confident. Usually, the anticipation produces the fear of failure and rejection. If you feel nervous, don't despair. You're normal! Three things will help you develop confidence: preparation, experience, and prayer.

Preparation can raise your confidence level. As you prepare to lead your group, be sure to plan for spontaneous interaction. That may sound like an oxymoron, but relaxed fellowship time will help people develop relationships, and thereby accomplish one of the biggest needs in people's lives, affirmation. Also, work on asking a few good questions. Don't overload your group with content, and end on time. Preparation doesn't mean that you cram in all the content you can. Remember that content is only one part of the group experience, and plan the interaction and fellowship adequately, too.

Nothing builds confidence like experience. Veteran group leaders have learned from many successes and failures. They fine-tuned their skills by leading many groups in many situations. Have realistic expectations of your leadership. The more groups you lead, the more confident you will become.

One more thing: Don't forget to pray. We may do the preparation, planning, and leading, but ultimately it is up to God to change lives. As Paul reminded the believers in Corinth:

> I planted, Apollos watered, but God was causing the growth.
>
> So then neither the one who plants nor the one who waters is anything, but God who causes the growth.
>
> 1 Corinthians 3:6–7

. . . YOUR PASTOR OR SMALL GROUP COORDINATOR SAYS YOU'RE NOT READY TO LEAD A GROUP.

Some of us may want to lead a group, but we may not be ready yet. Perhaps we haven't acquired the necessary skills; perhaps a tainted reputation prevents our assuming leadership; or perhaps we have not progressed far enough in our own healing process yet. Having someone tell us we aren't ready hurts, but it may save us from far deeper hurts of failing to lead well. Use the next several months or years to focus on the Lord and your own progress. As you grow, the Lord will use you in individuals' lives. After a while, you may be ready to participate in a team which is leading a group. Leadership is a privilege, not a right. Be patient with yourself, and with your pastor or coordinator.

. . . YOUR PASTOR ISN'T COMMITTED TO HAVING SUPPORT GROUPS IN HIS CHURCH.

Some pastors have had very negative experiences with support groups. Perhaps your pastor has had groups which caused division or attacked his leadership. Be patient with him. Listen to him. Share your desire to serve both him and the church by leading a group, and communicate your loyalty to the church. You may want to show him the Christ-centered books or training materials so he will understand that you are not going to lead a New Age-type group. You may ask him to meet with a Rapha representative or a small group coordinator from another church. Give him time to process this new information and then meet with him again. You may even ask him to sit in on the first group meeting.

. . . YOU HAVE TROUBLE GETTING STARTED.

Some of us have a difficult time overcoming initial inertia. Perhaps the fear of failure keeps us from doing the detail work of making announcements in Sunday school classes, putting announcements in the bulletin, calling prospective group members, setting the date for the first meeting, and getting started. If you are having trouble getting started, realize that the fear of failure is a common phenomenon. Talk to your small group coordinator. You may want someone to team-lead with you and share the responsibility.

Other factors which may inhibit the start of a group can include the time of the year (the period between Thanksgiving and Christmas is a very difficult time to start a group), lack of support from the church, poor timing of ads, and other logistical problems. Learn from difficulties and plan ahead as much as possible. But don't give up.

. . . YOUR GROUP DWINDLES TO TWO OR THREE PEOPLE.

Some of us have unrealistic expectations about the dynamics of groups. We invite four or five people, expecting each of them to attend the first meeting—as well as continuing to participate in our group until the Rapture! Experienced group leaders have a different perception. They realize that you usually have to personally invite 25 people for 15 to say they will attend. Of those 15, usually only eight to ten people will actually show up, and of those, only five to seven will be regular attenders after a month or so.

Other factors can cause groups to dwindle, too. Lack of child care, unresolved conflict in the group, holiday seasons, and poor preparation by the leader are some of these. Talk to your small group coordinator or a Rapha representative to get some insight and practical suggestions to help your group grow to a healthy size. Remember, quality usually produces quantity.

. . . YOUR GROUP BECOMES TOO LARGE.

When people find a supportive, nurturing environment and they are able to experience genuine healing, they usually invite their friends to join them. Outreach is a major emphasis of small groups. New members of a group are usually welcome in the first few weeks and some types of groups welcome new members throughout the course of the group. Other groups (such as sexual abuse groups), however, require such a high level of trust that it is very difficult to assimilate new members after the group has established open communication. After that point, the presence of new members may cause the group to regress, so be sure the new person can be trusted. When your group becomes too large, consider developing a new leader within the group and splitting into two groups. When new people want to join at inopportune times, ask them to wait until a new group is started.

. . . PEOPLE DON'T SEEM TO BE MAKING PROGRESS.

Virtually every group has people across the spectrum in their response to the material. Some seem to "click" and they grow rapidly. Others don't seem to catch on at all. Most are in between these extremes. Several factors prevent progress in people's lives, including:

- they may be afraid of being overwhelmed by all their repressed emotions;
- their denial may be so strong, they simply can't see reality yet;
- they don't trust the group members; or
- the material doesn't meet their needs.

Take some time to talk with these people individually and privately if they don't seem to be making progress after several weeks or months. Perhaps you'll find that they are actually learning more than you perceived. Perhaps you can help them determine the nature of their problems and help them take some steps. Remember that it is not your responsibility to make them grow. That is up to the Lord and them. Your responsibility is to provide a positive environment for that growth.

. . . THERE IS INTERPERSONAL TENSION OR CONFLICT.

Unresolved open conflict can kill a group—not just for that meeting, but completely. Similarly, unspoken tension saps the life from a group. Fellowship is one of the most important aspects of any group, but fellowship isn't just coffee and doughnuts. It is true Christian love: forgiveness, encouragement, correction, and caring. That kind of environment takes time to develop, but it is more powerful than any content. It is life-changing!

If conflict is openly expressed in the group, it is appropriate to resolve it openly. Use "I" words, and instruct others to use "I" words, too. If the conflict is between two members and is not brought out openly in the group, go to each one individually and then to both of them together to promote understanding, forgiveness, and reconciliation (see Matthew 18:15–17 and Galatians 6:1–2).

. . . MEMBERS OF YOUR GROUP BECOME DEPENDENT ON ONE ANOTHER OR GET INVOLVED WITH EACH OTHER SEXUALLY.

Support groups stimulate open communication of hurts and comfort of those wounds. Many people have never felt that kind of comfort and love before, and they are drawn to each other. Many leaders recommend that the group talk openly about their needs for affection and also, the necessity of setting boundaries on those needs. If you notice that two members are becoming too dependent on each others' affections or if you suspect sexual involvement, go to each of these people individually to share your concerns and listen.

Some group leaders jump too quickly to accuse people of interpersonal dependency or sexual involvement, but most group leaders err on the side of avoiding the conflict that can ensue from these discussions. Pray, talk to your small group coordinator or pastor, and go in love. Perhaps you misunderstood their communications, but perhaps your confronting them will save them years of heartache over poor decisions they are in the process of making now.

. . . SOMEONE IS UNUSUALLY QUIET IN THE GROUP.

To stimulate the involvement of quiet people, ask them non-threatening questions. You may ask them to tell facts about themselves: where they are from, their hobbies, what they do at home or at work, etc. After they communicate, move on to someone else. Don't make a big deal of their comments. After the meeting, you may want to talk privately with the quiet person, saying that you value his or her input in the group. At that point, the person may express fears of rejection and open the door for meaningful and cathartic communication between the two of you.

. . . SOMEONE WON'T STOP TALKING.

People who dominate a group by continuous talking can greatly hinder the spirit and progress of the group. Some techniques to divert the conversation from this person include:

- avoiding eye contact with him when he is talking;
- sitting next to him;
- interrupting when there is a pause in his speech—even a brief pause—and asking someone else's opinion;
- talking to him after the meeting. Communicate that you value his opinions, but that the goal of the group is for everyone to participate equally.

If trouble persists, tell the person that you will have to ask him not to come anymore if he cannot control his compulsion to talk. The good of the group takes precedence over one person's desire to be heard.

. . . SOMEONE IS OVERWHELMED BY ANGER, HURT, OR FEAR.

In the loving environment of support groups, repressed emotions often surface. People feel the long-festered hurts, anger, and fears of years of abuse and neglect, and sometimes these feelings are overwhelming. They may become violently angry, depressed, or unable to function in normal daily activities. Be sure to communicate the possibility of this phenomenon to your group members so they won't be caught off guard if it happens to them. When people are overwhelmed and need additional time, be sure to call your small group coordinator, local Rapha representative, or Rapha's national number (800/383-HOPE) to receive assistance and direction for the hurting person.

. . . SOMEONE GETS VERY ANGRY WITH YOU.

Quite often, a person in the healing process transfers his thoughts and feelings for someone else (typically a spouse or parent) to the person trying to help him. The helping person or counselor in some way represents the father, mother, sibling, or some other person important to the one being helped. Such representation, called transference, can be positive. For instance, a person may say to the helper, "You understand me better than my father ever did!" But sometimes this kind of representation is negative.

I once counseled a man who ascribed to me the characteristics of his neglectful father. He became quite angry with me and accused me of not caring for him. While helping another person through the healing process, it is important to expect this kind of behavior. If I hadn't been aware that anger is a common response in these situations, I might have begun to treat him the way his father treated him!

This kind of response by a helper or counselor to the person's attitude toward him is called counter-transference. Sometimes the helper may get caught up in the appreciation expressed by the one he is helping. Other times, he may become angry because the person isn't as responsive as the helper feels he should be. In either case, the helper or counselor has lost some objectivity in the relationship.

Transference on the part of a group member is normal. It allows the person to feel previously repressed emotions and verbalize hidden fears, hurt, and anger. But if the helper is unexpectedly blind-sided by another's transference, he can react very negatively, short-circuit the process, and damage the relationship.

. . . THE GROUP BECOMES INGROWN.

When people experience warmth and affirmation for the first time, they sometimes become protective of these relationships. When the group becomes ingrown, it loses one of its purposes—outreach. One way of keeping the balance of fellowship and outreach is to always have an empty chair in the group, symbolizing the group's commitment to reach out to new people who might fill that chair the next week. Other ways of emphasizing outreach include:

- having a pot-luck dinner and asking members to invite a friend who may want to join the group;
- praying for people—specifically or generally—who need the environment of a support group;
- talking monthly about the balance of fellowship, content, and outreach; and
- being an example to others: when a new person comes to the group, take the initiative to welcome him and get to know him.

Evaluation Questions

1. Which of these difficulties have you encountered in the past? What did you do about it? What were some of the results?

2. Which of these difficulties do you anticipate giving you the most trouble? Why?

3. What are some resources (people, seminars, training, literature, etc.) to help you?

How to Get Started

OBJECTIVE

- to provide a clear and simple plan to get groups started well.

PRAY THROUGHOUT THE STEPS outlined below. You will be working hard to insure an effective group, yet God must work in people's hearts. You must not trust in your own efforts but in God's involvement. Pray that He will guide your decisions and change people's hearts.

Week One - *Planning the Group*

1. Meet with your pastor or church group coordinator to review the group and to determine your role in it. A good way to do this is to review together the following group leader criteria:

   - desire for ministry with people dealing with the issues upon which the group will focus;
   - personal experience in dealing with the issues upon which the group will focus (this is especially true for those who desire to facilitate a support group);

- personal experience in a group and/or completion of a group leader's training program;
- spiritual maturity and a willingness to submit to the leadership of the church staff;
- teachable spirit;
- ability to provide elements of a successful group; and
- qualities/skills of a group leader.

2. Identify potential co-leaders as well as any other individuals who might be interested in joining the group.

3. Determine the topic for the group.

4. Determine whether the group will be open or closed.

5. Determine when the group will start and when and where it will meet. Keep in mind the elements in Setting the Stage.

6. Develop a strategy for publicizing the ministry to the church.

7. Order the materials needed. (Call Rapha Customer Service at 1-800-460-HOPE).

Week Two - *Publicizing the Group*

1. Place an announcement in the church bulletin.

2. Make an announcement from the pulpit. If possible, include a brief testimony by the group leader. His comments should identify the features and benefits of the group.

3. Plan at least one announcement as a bulletin insert. Include a description of the group and the date, time, and place of the first meeting. Also, note if child care is provided and include a form for people to sign up. List the group leader's name and phone number for further information.

4. Church-wide events can be scheduled to develop greater congregational awareness. Possibilities include:

   - a showing of *The Search for Significance* video series (this four-part series explores how we can base our self-worth upon the love, forgiveness, and acceptance of Jesus Christ, rather than upon our success and ability to please others);
   - a panel discussion on the topic of the group during a Sunday evening program; or
   - a sermon relating to group ministry in general or to the specific topic of the group.

Week Three - *Contacting Interested Individuals*

1. Contact (either in person or by phone, never through the mail) individuals who respond to announcements about the group.

2. Begin to develop a list of individuals to be involved in your core group. Based upon your situation, it is wise to have two to three individuals who meet the same criteria for group leadership listed above.

3. Determine if anyone in your group needs child care. Either arrange for child care at the church nursery, or put together a list of reliable baby sitters for members to call and arrange their own child care.

4. Visit the location for the group to plan the seating, temperature, and lighting. You may need to set up signs directing people to the room or house you will use.

5. For support groups:
   Begin to develop a list of individuals to form the nucleus of each group. Based upon your situation, it would be good to have several individuals who meet the following criteria:

- in the chemically dependent group, sobriety of one year or more;
- in the anorexia, bulimia, compulsive overeating, or codependency groups, significant progress in setting healthy limits and developing healthy relationships;
- participation in a support group; and
- a burden for the group program.

These people will not necessarily be co-leaders of the group, but their progress will provide modeling and encouragement for others who are beginning their recovery process.

6. Prepare for your first meeting. See the worksheet.

Week Four - *Begin Your Group*

1. Arrive early for your group to arrange the seating, temperature, and lighting. Also, set up any refreshments and music.

2. Call anyone who did not attend but who said they would like to. Encourage them, letting them know that you think the members of the group would enjoy getting to know them.

3. Your group may start small. As the word spreads, however, additional people will want to attend. View the initial group as an opportunity to learn and make necessary adjustments. Plan to add other groups as the leadership becomes available.

4. For support groups: establish accountability

   - Begin a same-sex buddy system. People are more likely to apply what they learn and maintain their commitment to the group and to sobriety if they are encouraged by someone. Consider pairing people by the second or third week so they can pray for one another, encourage one another, and strengthen the relationships in the group.

- Also, encourage group members to select a temporary sponsor until they are able to choose a permanent sponsor. These sponsors may be found in the groups or other community groups. Each person, then, would have a buddy and a sponsor. A sponsor is someone who:
  - has a sponsor of his or her own;
  - has been in the recovery process for approximately two or more years;
  - is a role model for recovery;
  - guides the group member through the 12-Steps or other material;
  - is a friend and a source of loving support; and
  - understands and respects the principle of anonymity.

An effective sponsor:

- will not give advice, rescue, or fix the group member;
- will not act as a therapist;
- will not break anonymity by sharing confidences with others;
- will not give harsh or shaming criticism; and
- will not neglect his or her own personal recovery in order to attend to the group member's needs.

Sharing leadership provides an opportunity for all the group members to feel ownership of the group and, therefore, feel accountable to the group and responsible for its ongoing success. It is important to delegate part of the leadership team. After all, each member's recovery is at stake if the group should fail.

Publicity

PUBLICITY TO ENLIST GROUP LEADERS AND FACILITATORS

The first objective in publicizing your new support group ministry will be to generate initial awareness of the groups and to enlist growth group leaders. This total process should take place one to two weeks prior to the group leader training session. To promote support groups, we recommend announcements in the church newsletter, Sunday school classes, and from the pulpit.

SAMPLE BULLETIN ANNOUNCEMENT

> Get involved and grow! In a few short weeks, our church will begin a support group ministry where you can experience an atmosphere of learning and sharing. WE NEED LEADERS AND FACILITATORS! If you would like to participate in this exciting ministry, please contact the church office and attend the Group Leader Training Session on (day of the week and date) at (time) a.m./p.m.

PUBLICITY TO INVITE GROUP MEMBERS

The objective of the second phase of growth group publicity will be to give specific information about the groups that have been organized. Promotion should include another set of bulletin inserts as well as announcements for the newsletter, Sunday school classes, and the pulpit.

We often recommend that churches begin their support group ministry with *The Search for Significance* groups. Here is a sample announcement for that purpose:

> Be a part of our support group ministry of fellowship and sharing. We will be working our way through the book, *The Search for Significance*, dealing with issues such as self-esteem and relationships. Learn how God can provide effective solutions for your life. Come join us and grow!

The Search for Significance led by (name of speaker)
First meeting will be on (day of the week and date), at (time) a.m./p.m. at (the home of (hostess/host's name or in Room _#_ of the ______ building).

If your church is starting several types of growth and support groups, you may want to use this announcement:

Sample Bulletin Announcement

Our church has a new support group ministry. Many people in our church and our community suffer from hurt, anger, manipulation, and strained relationships [You may want to list the types of groups your church offers, such as codependency, chemical dependency, anorexia, bulimia, sexual abuse, grief, etc,]. These groups offer an environment of affirmation and confidentiality where people can experience God's love and strength. Come join us . . .

TOPIC, led by __________.
Meeting on (day of the week and date) at (time) a.m./p.m., at the home of _________________(or in Room _#_ of the _________ building).

Evaluation Questions

1. Examine the plan carefully. What elements do you need to modify? Why?

2. Do you need help in getting started? If so, who or what are some resources to help you?

3. What is your schedule for accomplishing your plan?

Appendix

RESOURCES . . .

. . . for group coordinators, trainers, leaders, facilitators, members, and pastors.

RAPHA OFFERS a wide variety of resources to train, encourage, and equip churches so that their groups provide nurturing and healing environments. These resources include:

Training Material

Rapha's Trainers' Manual for Growth and Support Groups contains structured notes for the trainers as well as reproducible handouts for the new leaders of facilitators. The manual is designed so that the format can be a one-day seminar with two follow-up sessions, or a 12-week series.

Right Step Facilitator's Trainer's Manual and its corresponding videos are particularly designed to train facilitators for chemical dependency and codependency groups.

Additional Resources for Leaders and Facilitators . . .

Rapha has two books which are designed to help people understand the healing process and how they can help others in their recovery.

Getting Unstuck can be used in either an advanced growth group or in a support group. Group leaders can use it as a resource to understand why people have difficulty taking steps in their process.

Close Enough to Care is designed to help people understand how to help others struggling with emotional, spiritual, and relational difficulties. Both of these books are valuable tools for leaders and facilitators.

GROWTH GROUP MATERIALS

The Search for Significance teaches us how to base our self-worth upon the love, forgiveness, and acceptance that comes through Jesus Christ.

Your Parents and You and its accompanying workbook will enable you to analyze how your perceptions were shaped by your parents. Using Scripture, you will learn how to reshape false perceptions of God and yourself so that you can experience His love, forgiveness, and power in all of life's circumstances.

Codependency: A Christian Perspective offers sound biblical processes that promise hope and healing from the painful effects of codependency: the compulsion to rescue and control others.

Getting Unstuck helps those who are bogged down in recovery to uncover the "unfinished" business from their past and discover how it profoundly affects their relationships, thoughts, feelings, and behavior.

Conquering Fear will help you untangle the mysteries behind your emotional overload and teach you healthy ways to express your emotions through actual case studies and God's healing power.

Kidthink offers hope to the baffling task of understanding kids and dealing with their six most common behavioral patterns. To meet your child's needs and handle negative behavior effectively, you must learn to see the world through your child's eyes.

Relief for Hurting Parents helps you determine what to do and what to think when you're having trouble with your kids.

SUPPORT GROUP MATERIALS

Beyond the Darkness can deliver victims of sexual abuse from their haunting feelings and memories with its clearly communicated principles of recovery. They can learn to appropriately grieve the pain, learn to let go of the past, and reclaim trust, control, and intimacy.

Rapha's 12-Step Program for Overcoming Codependency is a combination of charts, self-tests, personal questionnaires, and self-paced inventories. This "workbook process" is a rewarding step on the codependent's road to lasting recovery and a healthy, productive life.

Rapha's 12-Step Program for Overcoming Eating Disorders tackles the compulsive-addictive patterns in which a person uses food in an emotionally or physically abusive way, and it presents an ongoing process for effective and permanent change from the debilitating disorders of anorexia, bulimia, and compulsive overeating.

Rapha's 12-Step Program for Overcoming Chemical Dependency leads chemically dependent people in a clinically tested, biblically-based, self-paced program to:

acknowledge their powerlessness; make sound judgments, understand the part their families have played; depend on God to resolve their boundary and responsibility issues; handle guilt, and much more.

Rapha's Step Studies for Overcoming Sexual Addiction will benefit those who struggle with pornography, exhibitionism, voyeurism, incest, rape, or child molestation or any other form of sexual addiction. This unique material helps people overcome denial, grieve the deep wounds they have experienced, repent of harmful behavior, and begin to develop healthy relationships.

Rapha's Step Studies for Overcoming Chemical Dependency condenses the content of our chemical dependency 12-step program into four pages per step to encourage a sense of progress, accomplishment, and responsibility.

Recovering From the Losses of Life shows us how to respond to life's inevitable losses in a positive manner by offering insights, keys from God's Word and the author's own experiences. You'll learn how to take charge of loss, face problems in grief and recovery, and adapt to the new roles that come with change. This practical and encouraging book will help you make all the transitions necessary for moving through a season of loss to a season of tremendous spiritual growth.

The Complete Divorce Recovery Handbook is designed to take you from the first moments of shock and grief to the process of inner healing and wholeness. Field-tested by hundreds of divorced people, it details a recovery program suitable for both small group discussions and individual use.

Hotlines

GROUP LEADERS' HOTLINE

If you have problems with your group and you need help, first contact your church's Group Coordinator or pastoral staff. If you still need help or if you have someone in your group who needs professional help, call Rapha's Group Leaders' Hotline at 1 (800) 383-HOPE.

MINISTERS' HOTLINE FOR COUNSELING ASSISTANCE

Rapha has established a toll-free ministers' assistance line, staffed by professionals who can assist the minister in those critical counseling situations, or perhaps be a helping hand to a minister who faces personal or family-related problems. When a minister has the opportunity to broaden his or her counseling resources, everyone benefits. Also, when ministers find healing for their own hurts and a new freedom in Christ, they can give their people a new dimension of hope out of their own experiences. Ministers may call 1-800-383-HOPE, 24 hours a day, seven days a week and receive counseling assistance.

Catalog

We are continuing to produce new materials for groups. For a free catalog of our growth group, support group, and training materials, call 1 (800) 460-HOPE.